ibiza style

Ingrid Rasmussen
Chloe Grimshaw

ibiza style

MERRELL
LONDON · NEW YORK

Introduction

It took us a year to find the most beautiful fincas and the most glamorous villas in Ibiza. We explored every part of the island, driving down endless dirt tracks (*caminos*), through acres of pine forests and up steep cliffs, to discover the definitive Ibiza style. We came to realize that there are two very different sides to Ibiza: a glamorous clubbing scene and a relaxed rural way of life. Few people pause to think that there is life beyond Amnesia, Pacha and Manumission, the clubs that made Ibiza infamous in the 1990s. The unspoilt countryside, filled with orange and lemon groves, wild-flower meadows and fields of fig trees, is the unexpected side of the island. Our aim was to unearth the stylish homes and exclusive hideaway hotels, known only to locals and the discerning traveller.

Artists, musicians and writers love the 'boho' feel of Ibiza. They first came to the island in the 1950s and 1960s, to hang out with the likes of Nico,

Terence Stamp, Charlotte Rampling, The Beatles and The Rolling Stones. Forty years later the appeal of the island is still as strong and it continues to attract the world's most glamorous DJs, models and photographers, including Kate Moss, Elle Macpherson, Jade Jagger, Eva Herzigova, Patrick Demarchelier and Mario Testino. It was in the 1960s that Ibiza's reputation as a hedonist's playground first took hold, as the hippy generation stopped off here en route to Goa and Bali. Bohos and beatniks arrived at dawn on the overnight boat from Barcelona to watch the sun rise above Ibiza Town. Looking for an alternative way of life, some ended up staying, and hippies, writers, musicians and artists moved into rural abandoned fincas (old farmhouses) to make their dream lifestyle a reality.

Until relatively recently, life for most Ibizans had remained unchanged for centuries. It was a simple rural community, living in homes with no mains water, little electricity and no gas, relying on wells for fresh water and charcoal fires for cooking. There were few cars on the island; instead, people travelled by horse-and-cart on the dirt roads. In the 1970s and 1980s it was still possible to purchase abandoned, run-down fincas fairly cheaply, but prices have risen sharply and are now on a par with those of the London property market and some of the most expensive properties in Europe.

Some Ibizan families have turned their farms into agroturismo hotels. Atzaro is one such conversion (pp. 98–103), now a sophisticated country hotel and spa, surrounded by acres of orange groves. Criss-crossing the island is a network of *caminos* that wind through the forests and fields to end up at extraordinary modern white houses and old stone fincas. The most likely location for a millionaire's villa is at the end of a long, potholed track.

Can Marti (pp. 268–75) was the first agroturismo hotel to open in Ibiza, in 1997, and there are now over twenty agroturismos across the island. These small and intimate hotels usually have between six and twelve individually decorated guest rooms. Many of the agroturismo fincas are over one hundred years old, and were often part of a larger agricultural estate. Most still have their own fruit trees and vegetable gardens, which now supply the hotel kitchens with fresh produce. Located in the depths of the countryside, miles from the nearest village, these hotels are often incredibly difficult to find, but that is part of their charm.

Boutique hotels are similarly bijoux, but they tend to have a more contemporary, minimalist aesthetic behind their design, with white walls, polished concrete floors and sophisticated bathrooms with power showers. Sculptural gardens are filled with spiky aloe vera, palms and cacti, and softened with swathes of bougainvillea and feathery olive trees. These chic bolt-holes are designed to cater for stressed urban visitors: Los Jardines de Palerm (pp. 216–21) offers calm white surroundings, Les Terrasses (pp. 182–91) is decorated in soothing blue and white, and Solibudha (pp. 206–15) is designed to have a Zen minimalist appeal.

Ibiza now has a hugely cosmopolitan population, including residents from France, Spain, Germany, Italy, The Netherlands, Argentina and Britain, and among them a fair share of eccentrics and alternative types. Ibizans, with their tolerant and easy-going attitude, have let these incomers set the tone for the whole island.

Ibiza was first settled in 654 BC, by the Carthaginians, who named it Ibossim, from the Phoenician *ibshim* (island of pines), and founded Ibiza Town. The Carthaginians came here to worship Tanit, their female goddess of the earth and fertility. Perhaps it is no coincidence, then, that the island tends to attract strong, independent women. Having been occupied by the Carthaginians, the Romans, the Byzantines and the Moors, Ibiza was conquered by the Catalans in the thirteenth century. For centuries, Ibiza has been celebrated as a healing, spiritual place; there are no poisonous plants or animals on the island, and its red earth is traditionally believed to have magical properties.

Using technology installed by the Moors, the Ibizans went on to become the biggest salt producers in the Mediterranean, trading with Spain and Italy. During the Renaissance, the Ibizans developed Ibiza Town, and surrounded it with a 2-kilometre (1-mile) stone wall. Their fortunes started to decline in the nineteenth century with the collapse of the salt trade, and in the twentieth century the Spanish Civil War caused devastation. When the hippies and travellers started to arrive in the 1950s and 1960s, the Ibizans welcomed them and recognized that the burgeoning tourist trade could revive their economy.

During the civil war many Ibizans had left the island, leaving behind them deserted fincas that the new arrivals were quick to make their homes. The oldest fincas in Ibiza date back to the seventeenth century. Then, Ibizan farms would have had a large central finca (the farmhouse), surrounded by smaller buildings, *corralles* (stables) and barns. The largest houses had one vast living and dining room, which could have a ceiling 6 to 9 metres (20 to 30 feet) high, and be double that in width, often with a large decorative arch spanning the room. Ledges and benches were built out from the walls, for storage and seating.

Fincas were constructed with thick stone walls, sometimes more than 1 metre (3 feet) wide, to keep the interior cool in summer and warm in winter.

For the same reason, windows and doors tended to be very small, meaning that traditional fincas are darker inside than most modern buildings. The dimensions of the old buildings were measured out using arm lengths for the width of windows and doors, and body height for verticals. Ibizans worked with building materials from the surrounding land, using rough stones for the walls, smooth flat stones for the floors, and sabina wood for the roof beams. Walls were painted white, inside and outside, with a limewash solution made from local chalk. If you look closely at these old buildings, between the roof beams you can often still see bits of shell and seaweed, which was used for insulation. Sabina (a cross between pine, cyprus and juniper) is still much prized for building today and is believed to have a greater tensile strength than steel. It grows slowly, and trees have to be at least eighty years old before they are tall enough to be used for roof beams.

Today, unless there is an existing building on the proposed site, it is almost impossible to build a new house in Ibiza's countryside, owing to strict planning regulations. For this reason, many of the modern villas have been constructed around crumbling old fincas. Architects have had to become highly inventive, and this, together with a desire to use local materials, has inspired such stylish new homes as the White House, built into the cliffs at

Es Cubells, with its curved wall of honey-coloured stone (pp. 54–59). One modernist white villa, Can Tia Den Roig, was designed to incorporate the ancient terracing of the old finca, with dramatic white spaces built to contrast with the rustic feel of the house (pp. 222–29).

A renewal of the traditional connection with the land is a growing trend in Ibiza, with many new residents wanting to live in an environmentally friendly way. Organic farms are springing up across the island, such as Can Marti, which sells organic produce to locals. On their property, Anabel and Barnabas Kindersley have planted a huge olive grove with 650 trees, which they farm organically (pp. 248–55). On a smaller scale, many residents are starting to establish their own organic vegetable gardens. The north of the island is still predominantly a farming community, with crops of oranges and lemons twice a year, and thousands of almond, olive and fig trees.

Life on the island is not, of course, confined to the busy summer months, and residents love the quieter feel of the autumn. The Parisian owners of the chic boutique hotel Solibudha explained why this is their favourite time of year: "In October or November the light is fantastic, with bright blue skies and crisp, clear days, whereas in August the sky becomes almost white because of the heat." Christmas and New Year herald a great series of parties and socializing, before the island's residents depart for warmer climes, with Indonesia, Bali and Goa being the favoured destinations of many. They return with hand-made furniture and textiles, bringing back something of the atmosphere of the countries they have visited to their Ibizan homes. For a change of scene, many Ibiza residents travel to Morocco to explore the architecture, souks and bazaars, and to stock up on handmade textiles, ceramics, lanterns and tiles.

Whether their home is a cool modern villa or a rustic finca, all the residents of Ibiza featured in this book share a common outlook and love the alternative lifestyle on the island, where anything goes. They have developed their own take on rustic chic by updating traditional fincas to become stylish hotels or luxurious country houses. Dynamic individuals have created distinctive contemporary homes, choosing open-plan living spaces, unified with polished concrete floors and floor-to-ceiling windows. Interiors seamlessly blend with exterior spaces, with rooms opening out on to shady terraces and gardens becoming outdoor rooms. Ibiza has a uniquely relaxed style: island life is all about lounging on daybeds or in hammocks strung between palm trees, surrounded by bougainvillea-shaded terraces, ancient olive trees and fragrant orange and almond groves.

coastal chic

Le Cabañon

On a boat trip around the north-west coast of the island, Françoise Pialoux glanced up at the cliffs of Ses Fontanelles and spied her ideal beach house. It was, she says, "an exceptional setting at the end of the world, with amazing sunsets". The architect who lived there was willing to sell the house to her, and she moved here in 1996.

Françoise was busy working on opening her first hotel in Ibiza, Les Terrasses, and had been keen to find a home of her own. Only houses on the north and west of the island can enjoy the famous Ibizan sunsets, and, built into the cliffs at Ses Fontanelles, Le Cabañon is perfectly sited for these breathtaking views. The house is built around a sculptural swimming pool, with a guest house on the lower level; steps lead up to the main house with its long, wide terrace overlooking the ocean.

The mountain boulders and pine trees were incorporated into the design of the house, providing shade for the pool and the terrace. The pool appears to merge with the ocean; as Françoise says, it is hard to tell where the pool ends and the sea begins. She designed stylish loungers to place around the pool and loves to relax here.

The colours throughout the house were inspired by those of the sky, and Françoise picked out soft greys and blues for the exterior, the terrace and the kitchen. She tends to spend most of her time outdoors, enjoying

LEFT, TOP A view of Le Cabañon's wooden terrace perched on top of a rocky outcrop and surrounded by the pine forest.

LEFT, BOTTOM Sun loungers designed by Françoise are perfectly positioned to take in the view out to sea from beside the infinity pool.

OPPOSITE A table on the terrace provides outdoor eating space for ten months of the year, with the views over the cliffs of Ses Fontanelles as a backdrop.

ABOVE, LEFT Françoise re-covered an old sofa in crisp white cotton and put up canvas blinds to create a cool, airy feel in the living room.

ABOVE, RIGHT A vintage table holds favourite books and magazines, as well as a sculpture of the Buddha and one made from shells, starfish and driftwood.

the year-round sunshine, and her favourite spot is on the terrace, which she imagines to be like "the wooden terrace of a colonial house". For meals, Françoise chose a large wooden table from Lorenzina in Ibiza, and folding canvas director's chairs, to accommodate all her family and friends, and has hung a stainless-steel hurricane lamp from the roof. An outdoor heater enables her to eat outside for all of the ten months of the year that she lives here, while netting and buoys collected from the beach below create a nautical feel.

Françoise loves cooking, and custom-designed the kitchen, which is on a raised area leading from the living room. It has a white-painted wooden floor and blue-grey rail, to echo the terrace outside. Just below the kitchen is an antique wooden table, where Françoise keeps striped tablemats and napkins in a wooden bowl.

On hot nights, Françoise sleeps on a large daybed out on the terrace, beneath a mosquito-net canopy. To keep the house cool during the day,

she has draped white muslin curtains from the roof beams of the terrace, and covered the full-height glass windows with white canvas blinds.

Keen to introduce Ibizan elements to the house, Françoise installed a white polished-concrete basin and shower in her bathroom. She wanted her bedroom to be clean and uncluttered, with all her possessions hidden away in blue-painted lattice-fronted cupboards. The only decorative elements are a bedcover from Lorenzina and four small pictures by Emily Trevena.

Françoise had lots of furniture made for Les Terrasses, her hotel, and picked some of the pieces for her home. She had the wooden coffee table made for the living room and re-covered an old sofa with crisp white cotton. A sculpture made of shells picks up on the beach theme. The guest house, which accommodates a constant stream of visitors in the summer months, was designed in the same simple, chic style as the private areas, with a polished-concrete floor, white bedcovers and driftwood lights.

ABOVE, LEFT Steps to the right of the blue-grey wooden rail lead from the living room up into the raised kitchen.

ABOVE, RIGHT The kitchen table is rarely used (except to hold a bowl of placemats and a basket of fruit), as the family like to eat outside all year round.

Casa Inspiration

Roland Walti's house is an eyrie made of glass, situated at the top of a mountain and overlooking the sea. The breathtaking view takes in the rocky outcrop of Es Vedra, a tiny island almost 3 kilometres (2 miles) out to sea that has many mythical associations. Roland, who likens his story to that of Odysseus's entrapment by the sirens of Es Vedra, sailed to Ibiza from England about thirty years ago, and for the first twelve years lived on his boat, before discovering this mountaintop site.

Having found a plot of land, Roland needed to build a house for his imminent family, as his girlfriend was expecting a baby. His aims were to "build a little house, to have water, a kitchen, a bathroom and a bed, and also to get the baby born in the house". The result was a small blue house, but his dream remained – to have a house made of glass, overlooking the sea. Before starting to design the new house, Roland spent a year observing the sunrise and sunset. Now, he says, "this is the only house

LEFT, TOP AND CENTRE The curved shape of the pond on the terrace echoes the form of the undulating concrete roof-line and folding glass walls of Casa Inspiration.

LEFT, BOTTOM The swimming pool is surrounded by paving that forms a striking pattern, and is perched on the cliff edge to make the most of the dramatic views.

OPPOSITE This view of the terrace shows the large sliding glass doors that open to blend the indoor and outdoor living spaces. The overhanging roof is a terrace, which becomes a dance-floor for Roland's legendary parties.

LEFT Low daybeds on a wooden platform built into the
cliffs are perfectly placed to enjoy the views of Es Vedra,
an island off the coast of Ibiza with mythical associations.

in Ibiza from where you can see the sun rise and set over the sea all the year. The same with the moon and the stars."

Roland's glass house is made up of a series of platforms and terraces set into the cliff. Outdoor staircases built into the rock connect the rooms with one another and lead to further bedrooms and living spaces beneath the main house. The flat roof functions as a huge terrace and above this is a small wooden hut, built from a mix of pine and driftwood, like a beach hut perched on top of a cliff.

The front door of the house is flanked by two huge sculptures from Borneo – figures of a man and a woman brought here by Roland to watch over the entrance. The main living space is completely open-plan, with the bed partially hidden behind white curtains. The polished-concrete bath and sink emerge organically from the wall, which is made from roughly hewn local red stone. The room is divided by a long, polished wooden surface, which functions both as the dining table and the kitchen

OPPOSITE Visible in the reflection on the large sliding glass windows is the industrial stainless-steel fence along the edge of the terraces, which provides safety without obscuring the view.

ABOVE Teak daybeds are placed in the corner of the living room, overlooking the terrace and the views out to sea, around Roland's home-made coffee table.

worktop. Made from Brazilian hardwood and lacquered with ship's varnish, it resembles the deck of a boat. At the far end of the room is space to sit and talk and take in the view, with daybeds arranged around a sculptural wooden coffee table. The daybeds were made by a friend using recycled teak and the supports were made from Indonesian wooden ploughs, once used to till rice fields. The coffee table is formed from an intricately carved Indonesian sculpture, which Roland customized by adding wheels and a glass top.

Like many people in Ibiza, Roland and his partner, Carolina Paredes, live quietly for most of the year, the rhythm of their lives controlled by the sun's rising and setting over the sea. But during the summer months they hold huge parties on the terrace, entertaining up to five hundred people at a time. The location of the house and its proximity to Es Vedra are a constant source of inspiration to Roland, as reflected in the name he has given his home. Casa Inspiration is a work in progress, evolving and changing with its owner's creative impulses, and growing as he creates new platforms, rooms and terraces for his glass eyrie.

LEFT, TOP The rough stone of the walls and floors contrasts with the smooth plaster finish of the bathroom, which forms an elegant corner in the house.

LEFT, BOTTOM An Indonesian wooden four-poster bed is screened from the main living area by sheer muslin curtains.

La Casa Che Canta

Dutch architect Jan Wichers bought a plot of land on Ibiza's east coast in 1970, but it was not until thirty years later that he was able to build a house on the site. He and his wife, Italian journalist Cristiana, escape to Ibiza as often as they can, and have a shared appreciation of good design and relaxed living. Jan has always loved the simplicity of life here: "There is something else to the island, something very special; once you leave the main roads, you find yourself in very simple countryside."

The only sign of La Casa Che Canta seen from the road is a rusty metal *toro*, resembling a Picasso sculpture of a bull, perched high on top of a wooden fence. Viewed from the drive, the house seems rather austere at first, with a long terracotta wall and a double-height front door. It is not until rounding the corner to the terrace that the entire building is revealed. To make the most of its clifftop location, Jan wanted the front of the house to be completely open to the sea, so he built terraces on both of its levels. Huge glass windows take full advantage of the view. "You come here to feel good," Jan says; "to enjoy the sun, the view and the sea breeze."

Jan wanted to create a certain flow between the different areas of the house, and chose not to have separate rooms with lots of doors, but instead to create open-plan spaces. Floor-to-ceiling windows on the ground floor open out on to the terrace, blurring the distinction between the interior and the exterior and between the living and dining areas. To unify the space, Jan chose large Turkish limestone tiles, which follow the same lines inside and out. The limestone was cut specially to fit the house, with larger tiles for the living areas and smaller tiles for the bathroom and staircase.

RIGHT This view of the house from the end of the infinity pool on the hillside shows how the sliding glass doors can create a seamless space of the terrace, living room and kitchen.

A small living area has been created by placing an Italian sofa opposite two Marcel Breuer chairs, with a curved glass table by Danny Lane for Phium, designed to look like waves of water. Jan bought the chairs with his first pay cheque and has taken them with him from home to home ever since. Next to the sofa is an angular wooden stool by Charles and Ray Eames, made from one piece of wood. Against the wall is a row of African metalwork pieces, items that were originally farm tools but have become twentieth-century sculpture. On the opposite wall, a row of clear and green wine-bottle necks mounted on glass creates an unusual coat rack. The young German artist who designed it used the rest of the bottles to make simple but stylish vases.

Jan did not want the kitchen to be hidden away behind doors; instead, it is the focal point of the house, where friends can talk and cook together. The cook looks directly out to sea, enjoying one of the best viewpoints that the house has to offer. During the summer, the dining table can be moved out on to the terrace.

Continuing the open-plan flow of the house, the bedroom leads off from the living room, and on to the terrace. A bathroom has been created

OPPOSITE, TOP LEFT The entrance is a contrast of textures, with a double-height wooden front door set into the rough Ibizan stone of the wall.

OPPOSITE, TOP RIGHT In the vintage-style guest room, a woven African bag is flung on a chaise longue, in front of an antique table from a Viennese coffee shop. The large colour photograph is by Sigrid Rothe.

OPPOSITE, BOTTOM, LEFT AND RIGHT In the kitchen, the wooden units were all made by Jan's cabinetmakers in Germany. A large photograph by Vietnamese artist Thái-Cong Quách and a pile of dishes add splashes of colour.

RIGHT, TOP The modern sculptures beside the antique chair were made from African farm tools.

RIGHT, BOTTOM A view of the infinity pool from the house.

by sectioning off part of the bedroom space with a waist-high wall. A sink has been fitted in the dividing wall, and behind this is a walk-in wardrobe, a shower and a lavatory. Cristiana and Jan both admire Italian design, and their elegant, modern Italian-designed bed is one of the key pieces they selected for their home. The translucent blue fan suspended from the ceiling is also a lamp, and is another Italian-designed piece. On the walls are black-and-white photographs by well-known German photographers, including Jochen Blume's portrait of Sophia Loren and Edmund Laufer's iconic image of Linda Evangelista.

For the downstairs guest bedroom, Jan sought out vivid patterns, including a colourful woven African bag and an old Persian Qashquai kilim. The chaise longue is called Nona Maria (Grandmother Maria), from Flex Form, and Jan picked up the antique table – possibly by Josef Hoffmann – from an old coffee house in Vienna. The centrepiece is a large colour photograph by German photographer Sigrid Rothe, who is famous for her close-up pictures of orchids in surreal colours.

Jan likes to escape from his busy architectural practice in Hamburg whenever he can. He used to be able to leave his work behind, but now more and more people are asking him to build houses on the island.

PREVIOUS PAGES, LEFT A low white wall separates the open-plan living room from the limestone staircase. On top of the wall is an oval wooden sculpture by Pino Pedano, and in front of the glass panel, a 'Le Violin' chair by Carla Venosta.

PREVIOUS PAGES, RIGHT These three wooden stools came from Bali and are made from burlwood, which is also used for making smoking pipes.

LEFT, TOP AND BOTTOM Doorways at the far end of the open-plan bedroom and bathroom lead into a dressing room and shower. The sink is fitted into the waist-high wall behind the head of the bed.

La Divina

Born in Madrid, Alejandro Castelbarco worked there as an investment banker until he decided to leave his job in order to pursue his real passion: designing and building houses. His job had taken him to Asia and South America, but, looking for a more relaxed way of life, in 2004 he exchanged his loft apartment in Madrid for a cool, modernist villa in Ibiza. He now avoids being in Ibiza in August but chooses to spend spring and autumn at La Divina, "sitting by the fireplace with a clear view out to Formentera".

Alejandro looked at more than sixty houses on the island before discovering this modernist concrete villa high in the hills, overlooking the sea. He was looking for the same type of low-level concrete house that he had seen in Bali and Mexico, with a similar relaxed feel. La Divina is a modern, angular villa built into the hillside, with overhanging terraces, sliding glass windows and an infinity pool. The house was only half-built when Alejandro found it, but he recognized its potential.

LEFT, TOP AND BOTTOM The modernist-inspired concrete villa is evocative of contemporary villas in Bali and Mexico.

OPPOSITE The heavy wooden door in the stone wall makes a dramatic entrance to the house, with a Balinese sculpture visible inside.

OVERLEAF, LEFT Alejandro found the low wooden tables for the living room in Bali, and bought the modern sofas in Ibiza, at La Maison de L'Elephant.

OVERLEAF, RIGHT One of the exterior walls of the house, made from roughly hewn Ibizan stone, has been left unplastered in the entrance hall. It creates a striking contrast to the clean lines of the interior walls.

When Alejandro bought the house, in springtime, he had the feeling that the Ibizan builders and plumbers did not see his project as a priority. Deciding to take matters into his own hands, he moved into the half-built property to start work himself, despite having no electricity or running water. Eventually, after two months, the local plumbers and electricians took pity on him and came back to finish the work.

Alejandro's concept of Ibizan style is to keep it simple: he loves the huge empty spaces in his house and feels that all you really need are a few interesting pieces of furniture and a few large daybeds. In the corner of the living area low sofas are aranged in an L-shape in front of the double-height windows, taking advantage of the view out to sea. The house is full of furniture that Alejandro has designed and worked on himself. His dining table is a modification of a design that he saw in Mexico, drew up himself, and had made in Bali, though he rather sadly admits it is a resounding failure because it is too tall and wobbles. A carpenter friend in Ibiza

helped him to build much of the furniture. From aroco wood that they found by the side of the road, a long, low table for Alejandro's books has been created; other pieces were used to make the wooden counters in the bathroom for an unconventional look. All the outdoor furniture is from Bali, from the wooden table and chairs on the terrace to the low wooden table next to the pool. During warm weather, Alejandro hangs a large white canopy from the top floor to create some much-needed shade and moves the daybeds outside to the terrace.

Alejandro wanted to install a smooth polished-concrete floor in his home but unfortunately the flooring had already been laid and was too expensive to replace. The original architect used the same stone throughout, with raw marble inside and on the terrace, and polished marble for the pool. Alejandro has learned to live with it and says, "I actually like the floor because it's all natural and I like the feel of it. The problem is that I'm not a marble type, I'm a polished-concrete type."

Throughout the house is an impressive collection of artwork: at the entrance there is a round wooden sculpture, which Alejandro found in Bali and has left outside to weather to a silvery grey colour, and upstairs there are huge sculptures that are made from palm trunks, painted and polished to achieve a burnished look. He reveals that he won the paintings of a black lady by an Argentinian artist "in a poker game in Costa Rica".

A perfectionist at heart, Alejandro still does not consider his Ibizan villa to be finished: he would like to add on more bedrooms, perhaps build a huge suite and find more pieces of furniture on his travels. He has also built properties in Bali and Colombia, but admits that he is always happy to come home to his place of refuge, his retreat in Ibiza, saying, "I don't think there is anywhere like the Balearic Islands elsewhere in the world."

OPPOSITE, TOP LEFT In the guest bedroom, the bed is hung with mosquito nets from Bali suspended from bamboo frames. Beside the bed are some large, burnished vessels made from palm tree trunks.

OPPOSITE, TOP RIGHT Alejandro designed the bathroom himself. He used reclaimed aroco wood and new fittings, with a ceramic sink and a glass-walled shower.

ABOVE Out on the terrace, furnishings are kept to a minimum, with only a low Balinese table and a white daybed, so as not to interrupt the spectacular views from the cliff-top terrace.

The White House

Seduced by just one weekend in Ibiza, Elizabeth Foster and her partner decided to make their home on the island in 1995. They discovered a fisherman's cottage, with no running water and accessed by a dirt road, but in a unique location, "perching on the mountain, overlooking the water", close to the magical rock of Es Vedra, which is reputed to give Ibiza its unique energy.

Elizabeth worked with Argentinian architect Victor Mendez, who shared her vision of creating a house that would capture the extraordinary ever-changing coastal light and make the most of the views of the rocky coves and sea below. Some of the walls of the original cottage were retained, but to create more outdoor space and make room for a swimming pool, Elizabeth realized that the only option was to demolish part of the mountain. As a result, she now has a dramatic curved wall alongside the infinity pool.

The White House is entered through a double-height front gate set into thick walls of Ibizan stone and giving access to a small courtyard with an ancient palm tree. A flight of stairs leads up from the front door to the living area, where Elizabeth wanted to re-create the Ibizan values of "easy living and nonchalance". The canvas deckchairs recline until they are almost horizontal, and there are white daybeds and comfortable white

LEFT, TOP AND BOTTOM Built into the side of the mountain, the White House has steep steps leading up through the courtyard from the tall gate, to a dramatic staircase that leads to the first floor.

OPPOSITE Part of the mountain was demolished to create the new terrace and infinity pool. Rocks at the corners of the pool are all that remain. A white awning provides much-needed shade, with low white sofas forming the perfect place for a siesta.

ABOVE, LEFT On a clear day you can see the island of Formentera from the terrace of the living room. White daybeds and canvas deckchairs provide places to recline while taking in the view.

ABOVE, RIGHT Elizabeth and her partner have an eclectic art collection, ranging from contemporary works to nineteenth-century French sculpture and pieces of African art.

sofas on which to relax. A long, narrow window frames the sea, sliding open to give an uninterrupted view. Orange-and-white glass vases picked up at the Conran Shop in London provide focal points of colour on the outdoor terrace.

Elizabeth and her French partner, who now have a three-year-old daughter, have gathered together a comprehensive collection of antiques, African art and vintage French posters, lithographs and drawings. Treasured pieces include a Matisse drawing and a first-edition Gustave Moreau lithograph. Racing memorabilia, including Michelin man posters and a Monaco Grand Prix print from 1931, adorn the spare bedroom, while in the living room a Lutheran Bible shares a table with an ancient stone bowl from Pakistan.

The open-plan dining room is home to classic pieces of modern design and a quirky mix of interesting objects and antiques: the huge jawbone of an elephant sits next to a pair of antique French candlesticks. On the wall

leading to the kitchen is a tapestry that dates from the 1850s and depicts the marriage of an Indian maharaja. The kitchen units are of blue-green frosted glass, echoing the colours of the bay, while above them is a row of polished-concrete shelving.

Polished concrete has been used throughout the house. In the guest bedroom, concrete forms the base of the bed, the bath and a natural, sloping sink; the room's flooring consists of pebbles set into concrete and painted white. The bedding echoes the theme of natural materials, with a bisque cable-knit cashmere blanket and Japanese white linen sheets. Elizabeth was keen to create "sexy Ibiza bedrooms", as the island seems to have a way of releasing inhibitions. Both her own and the guest bedroom contain a bath as well as a bed, giving "a very Ibiza feel".

In the corner of the master bedroom, set into the floor, is a round bath, from which you can see the sea. Elizabeth describes how "it feels as if you are taking a bath in the sea, and when you are lying in bed you feel

ABOVE, LEFT Every living space in the house has a view of the sea, and in the kitchen it is reflected in the colouring of the fittings on the wall opposite the view.

ABOVE, RIGHT This sculptural open fireplace is the main source of heating for the living room during the winter months.

as if you are floating out to sea". The furniture is another seemingly effortless blend of contemporary design and antique pieces, which include a gently faded nineteenth-century zebra-skin rug, a seventeenth-century Spanish writing desk and a 1940s wicker chair from Paris.

Breakfast is taken on the terrace outside, shaded from the bright Ibizan light by a canopy of banana trees. In the garden, Elizabeth has planted only tropical plants that can thrive in the harsh climate. The global theme of the interior furnishings continues outside, with an Indian throw in natural earth tones covering some white cushions, and with hand-crafted terracotta bowls from Africa. The seating area by the pool is covered with a giant awning, like a huge white sail.

The huge curved wall in the side of the mountain was designed to look as if a wave had rushed over it. Great quantities of honey-coloured Ibizan stone had to be carried up the mountain to create it, but a few original mountain rocks sit around the pristine white surface surrounding the swimming pool. Rows of deckchairs from the 1930s are arranged around the pool, lending a decadent *Great Gatsby*-like feel. The South American wood-and-cord tables and chairs have been left outside to bleach in the sea air and the sun.

Steps cut into the cliff lead down to a private creek below, from where you can swim in deserted coves or take a boat to explore Es Vedra. For a change of scene, Elizabeth sometimes jumps into her speedboat and arrives at the island of Formentera just fifteen minutes later.

RIGHT, TOP The guest room is an open-plan bedroom and bathroom. One side of the room has a bath and sink made from solid concrete.

RIGHT, BOTTOM Behind the 1930s deckchairs, the South American table and chairs made from wood and cord are visible against the stone wall.

Las Banderas

Visitors who take the ferry from Ibiza to Formentera will find a pace of life that is completely different: there are no clubs there, nor even a single traffic light. Hidden among the sand dunes on a windswept beach is Las Banderas, an eclectically decorated guest house that makes the perfect base from which to explore this wild and beautiful island.

Yvonne Van Dalsen, a fashion designer, bought Las Banderas in 1980. Although she no longer runs the hotel, she still keeps an apartment on the top floor, which has views along the beach and out across the turquoise sea. "Turquoise was always my favourite colour," she says, "and I always try to look for turquoise textiles or objects on my travels." Often travelling during the winter months, she has brought back furniture and sculpture for her home from such places as Bali and Burma.

In the living room, Yvonne has placed Art Deco-style sofas on opposite sides of the room to take full advantage of the sea views. In her typically bold style, she has covered the sofas with animal-skin fabric. A low wooden table was brought back from Essaouira in Morocco. Her turquoise and silver bedroom is furnished with a 1920s traditional silver-embossed bed from Andalusia, turquoise Indian wall hangings and a chandelier customized with blue stones. Yvonne likes to customize

LEFT, TOP The boldly coloured Las Banderas, glimpsed from the beach. The row of windows visible at the top is part of the owner's penthouse apartment.

LEFT, BOTTOM Outdoor living areas have a relaxed feel, with vintage bamboo-and-wicker chairs and Moroccan lanterns. Colourful silk drapes are hung from wooden posts and awnings.

OPPOSITE Guests at Las Banderas can wander up from the beach for cocktails and tapas under a straw sun-shade.

furniture to fit her bold colour scheme: the lacquered Chinese cupboard in her bedroom, for example, has been painted bright pink. The kitchen is dominated by an ornate carved-wood dining table and chairs from Bali, with a dramatic 1920s lamp from Buenos Aires hanging above.

Yvonne's friends Leah and John Tilbury took over the running of the hotel in 2001. It was a challenging project, as Las Banderas needed to be completely renovated. Being right on the seafront, the hotel has to be painted both inside and out every year to repair the damage caused by the salt in the wind and spray, but Formentera's stringent building laws mean that the couple need to obtain a licence even to change the colour of the walls.

Yvonne's first project, twenty years before Leah and John took over, had been to build the outdoor bar and terrace. The German builders she hired drank a great deal of beer, and every time they finished a bottle, they put it in the outside wall that they were building. The bottles create an amazing effect at sunset, when the sun shines through the wall and "all you can see is sunlight sparkling through the glass". Yvonne also designed the colourful ceramic mosaic-tiled floor for the bar and terrace, one of Leah's favourite parts of the hotel: "I love the tiling and I love the mismatch!" Leah and John carried on with the theme, tiling the winding stairs and corridors throughout the hotel with mosaics. Picking up on the idea of 'Las Banderas', Leah made huge flags or banners to put on the beach around the hotel: "We have strong winds here, and I love the way the flags look along the beach, billowing in the air."

OPPOSITE Vintage Moroccan fabric was used to make the cushions and tablecloths for the restaurant. Quirky pictures and a battered straw hat add to the hippy feel.

Las Banderas enjoys a relaxed beach atmosphere, and Jade Jagger often stays at the suite here, which has a four-poster bed that was Leah's wedding bed. A shell chandelier and a painted wicker chair give the suite a hippy-chic look. Double glass doors lead down into a small living room, with a separate bed and a curved wicker sofa that doubles as a daybed. Huge windows, hung with sheer drapes, give a view of the beach beyond.

Leah explains that a hotel is usually expected to be perfect, but she aimed to create a deliberately imperfect feel. For a bohemian look, she has hung the bar and restaurant with Moroccan lanterns and throws, and brightly coloured silk fabric has been made into cushions and wound around columns and benches. When Leah wanted to brighten up the dark interior of the hotel, she asked her father, Lance, an Ibizan artist, to come out to Formentera to decide on the colour scheme. Leah recalls: "My dad's quite a character and he came screaming down the beach shouting, 'I've got it, I've got it: we should do Neapolitan ice-cream!'" It has now become a family tradition to change the colours every year, "just to give it some oomph".

Las Banderas is the ultimate hippy-chic hideaway, with its ceramic mosaic floors, vintage furniture, Moroccan lanterns and quirky details. There is no name sign on the hotel, just a bunch of brightly coloured flags waving in the breeze.

LEFT, TOP This glamorous sitting area in the guest suite has a bohemian feel, with a vintage wicker sofa and a shell chandelier.

LEFT, BOTTOM The arched doorway and antique metal lantern create a Moroccan feel in this intimate bedroom. The simple furnishings include a metal-framed bed and white cotton sheets.

OVERLEAF, RIGHT A sculpture made from found objects greets you on your arrival at Las Banderas, giving a taste of the eclectic feel within.

rural retreat

Can Reco de sa Bassa

Isabella Gnecchi, former editor-in-chief of *Harper's Bazaar*, retired to Ibiza in search of a chic country retreat. She first visited the island in 1968, "at the end of the sixties, with the hippies", and returned in the late 1990s because she realized that "there's a togetherness of things here that is very rare and totally understated".

The four-hundred-year-old finca that Isabella discovered in Santa Agnes, a tiny village at the north of the island, was little more than a crumbling ruin, and it took four years to rebuild the house completely. Traditional techniques were used wherever possible: the polished-concrete floors, for example, were made, as in many old fincas, according to a method that originated in north Africa. Isabella described the process: "The floor is made up of layers of white concrete, sand and pigment. We used local sand and a little ochre to give colour to the floor, which is then polished frequently with beeswax."

An important influence that helped to shape the look and feel of the house was Isabella's friendship with the artist Grillo Demo, who has lived on the island for thirty years. His work can be seen throughout the house: in the living room, for example, a huge black-and-white photograph of Isabella has been transformed by Grillo Demo into a painting of falling jasmine, while his huge sculptural vase with coloured butterflies is carefully positioned on the glass table in the centre of the room.

LEFT, TOP Set amid the farmland of Santa Agnes, the restored finca is approached along a grassed-over stone path.

LEFT, BOTTOM The fragrant garden has been planted with rose geranium, oregano and lavender.

OPPOSITE Rows of navy-blue canvas-and-teak loungers surround the swimming pool, and are seen here from under the canopy of the olive grove.

ABOVE The large entrance hall has a polished-concrete floor and partially plastered walls that reveal the stonework of the old building. The open-sided staircase leads to Isabella's study and bedroom, and the roof-top terrace.

Isabella travels regularly to Kenya, where her brother lives, and collects pieces for her home: the sculptural wooden daybeds in the entrance hall, piled with cushions made from Indian silk saris, are from the Kenyan island of Lamu. A cosy living room opens off the hallway, designed to look like the wood-panelled drawing room of a hunting lodge, with its book-lined walls and sheepskin-covered sofas. Isabella used bleached-white elephant bones that she found in Africa as the focal point of a coffee table made from sabina wood; the bones are inside a glass-topped cavity within the table. Isabella's collection of sand dollars, symbols of good luck, from the beach in Lamu are in a tray on top of the table.

At the opposite end of the hall is the 25-metre (82-foot) kitchen and dining room, designed by Isabella as a relaxed space with a cooking island and an intimate seating area around the fireplace. French windows open out on to a shaded dining terrace, overlooking a fragrant garden filled with fig trees, rose geraniums, oregano and lavender. Guests can lounge

outside on daybeds made from rope and wood, and in armchairs made from coffee wood, all brought back from Lamu. In keeping with this easy-going atmosphere, cushions are covered in vintage tea towels and *kikoys* (Kenyan cotton pareos).

Isabella's bedroom on the first floor doubles as a salon, where friends and family can come to enjoy her favourite photographs, artworks and antiques. From her mother's house in the south of France, a collection of eighteenth-century antiques has found its way to Ibiza, including the elegant porcelain ducks on the marble side table, and the wooden mantelpiece. A life-size ceramic dog, reminiscent of the wild dogs of the island, stands on either side of the fireplace. An Aztec ceremonial sculpture, in the form of a bird's head, takes pride of place on the mantelpiece. Behind the bed are two figure-shaped ceramic opium pillows, on which opium smokers would originally have lain their heads. Every room in the house features works of art by Grillo, and the bedroom

ABOVE, LEFT The cosy living room resembles a wood-panelled hunting lodge, with book-lined walls, sheepskin-covered sofas and leopard-print cushions. Isabella displays favourite books and sculptures on the sabina-wood and glass coffee table.

ABOVE, RIGHT The open-plan kitchen was designed to be a sociable place, with a free-standing cooking island and space for cooking while entertaining friends.

is no exception, with two of his red velvet paintings displayed on the far wall, framed with wood found in Africa.

Three steps lead down from Isabella's bedroom to her study, which is decorated in a similar style to the bedroom, with personal finds mingling with valuable antiques. Here, a bowl of sea urchins collected on the beach sits next to an Art Deco sculpture by Max Le Verrier, while white shelves are used to display her collection of antique and vintage purple glass. Isabella has been collecting glass since the 1960s, and she has pieces that range in value from a few pence to thousands of pounds, and are as likely to have come from junk shops as from Liberty or Biba, or Guinevere on London's King's Road.

Isabella is perhaps most proud of the huge garden that she has created from scratch, and she clearly loves living in her rural surroundings. Over several years, she has planted olive and fruit trees, herbs and flowers. She has even made her own olive oil: having planted two hundred trees when she first moved to Can Reco in 2006, they "picked 500 kilos [1100 lbs] of olives and made 55 litres [14 gallons] of oil. The farmer pressed the olives in the traditional way, using an old stone press to crush them and baskets underneath to collect the oil as it leaked down."

LEFT, TOP The brushed-steel-framed twin beds in the guest room were designed in Paris in the 1950s. Between the beds is a nineteenth-century English '3-steps' trunk side table, and on top of this is a nineteenth-century Chinese bowl decorated with a snake design.

LEFT, BOTTOM Isabella collects old roses, taking cuttings from plants found in friends' gardens around the world. She particularly likes Meilland roses, in either delicate pale pink or very deep red.

OPPOSITE A window flung open over the roll-top bath looks out to the pine forest surrounding the house. Family photographs cover the walls behind Isabella's collection of sun-hats.

Cana Marina

Expert windsurfers Peter Whaley and his wife, Thérèse Suringar-Whaley, are two of the pioneers of the immigrant community in Ibiza, having moved here in the early 1980s. Peter opened one of the first bars in Ibiza Town and Thérèse established a sportswear shop next door, both named Graffiti. For their home, they found a three-hundred-year-old finca in the north of the island, and began its painstaking restoration with the assistance of local architect Rolph Blakstad.

The first steps were to restore the sabina-wood ceilings and to extend the original finca, to create another bedroom, a children's bathroom, an outdoor living room and a small guest house. Inspired by a visit to the Alhambra near Granada, Peter and Rolph went on to explore Morocco, researching the Moorish/Arab influence on Spanish culture. From this trip, they brought back antique tiles with which to decorate the outdoor living areas and terraces and create Moorish-style bathrooms.

The largest room in the house is the living room, which has sliding glass windows that open out on to the ponds, terraces and gardens; these windows can fold back to create an outdoor room. The long, narrow ponds are filled with water-lilies and the walled garden offers a cool respite from the summer heat. Inside the living room, traditional bench seating has been built out from the walls and covered with white and red

LEFT, TOP This view shows the Moroccan marble fountain and the rattan daybed placed next to the swimming pool. Behind them is an orchard of fruit trees.

LEFT, CENTRE AND BOTTOM Antique Moroccan tiles have been used to create the dramatic walled gardens.

OPPOSITE Outside the living room is a peaceful lily-pond, surrounded by walls that are screened with palm trees and bougainvillea.

cushions to create a comfortable lounge area. The old colonial-style wicker armchairs from India, which belonged to Peter's parents, have cool white cotton covers. Most of the furniture in the living room is from India, Burma and Morocco; in the last of these Peter also picked up the lanterns and paintings.

With two young children to consider, Peter and Thérèse decided to build a typical Ibizan kitchen and commissioned a large wooden table from a local carpenter. They had cushions made up in Bali to fit the surrounding chairs and benches. The Moroccan candlesticks were a present from a French photographer. A big bowl on the table contains lemons from the garden.

Peter and Thérèse's bedroom has a huge terrace that overlooks the gardens and is draped with bougainvillea. The styling of their bedroom was inspired by trips to Bali, and they had a local carpenter design the bed, with its bamboo frame hung with mosquito netting. The Moroccan-style bathroom has a deep arch above the recessed bath and is tiled with rich blue, green and white antique tiles picked out by Peter.

OPPOSITE, TOP RIGHT The large kitchen table and bench were made by a local carpenter. The cushion on the bench came from Bali and the Moroccan candlesticks were a present from a French photographer.

OPPOSITE, BOTTOM LEFT Traditional bench seating has been built against the walls of the living room and a large Balinese footstool is used as a coffee table. The cushions were embroidered by Victoria Durrer-Gasse.

LEFT, BOTTOM The design of the bed in the guest room was based on that of a Thai temple bed, and was made by a local carpenter. The bedcover is from India and the mosquito netting is from Bali.

Thérèse brought back mosquito nets for the house from Bali, including the net above the bed in the guest bedroom. The design of the bed was based on that of a Thai temple bed; Thérèse still likes to imagine monks sitting or sleeping on it. Carved wooden sculptures of birds and animals came from Expo 92 in Seville, where Peter managed to buy a whole truckful of wooden carvings from the New Guinea pavilion. There is also another old colonial chair from Peter's parents and a low wooden table from Morocco.

Peter and Thérèse have drawn on Moorish design to bring their once-derelict finca back to life. Their home, filled with textiles, paintings, furniture and sculptures brought back from their travels, is resonant with the many cultures that this island melting-pot has represented for thousands of years.

OPPOSITE, TOP LEFT The guest bathroom is approached through an arched corridor, which is illuminated by a glass lantern. On the far wall, the arch shape is complemented by an alcove behind the bath and the geometric design of the antique Moroccan tiles.

OPPOSITE, TOP RIGHT AND BOTTOM RIGHT Peter and Thérèse's bathroom is also decorated with Moroccan tiles, in deep green and blue, and the sink has Moroccan brass taps.

RIGHT, TOP Two colonial Indian wicker chaise longues have pride of place in the living room and are framed by arches leading out into the gardens. The lanterns and paintings in this room are from Morocco.

RIGHT, BOTTOM Arches in the Moroccan-inspired garden courtyards provide much-needed shade around the finca.

Casa Tipi

Serena Cook first visited Ibiza in 1996 and fell in love with the unspoilt countryside of the island, spending the summer in a rural finca, but it was not until 2001 that she closed her organic café business in London to take up Jade Jagger's invitation to cook at her three houses on the island. While working for Jade and as a freelance cook she realized the need for a concierge service and now spends half the year living in Ibiza, running her hugely successful business, Deliciously Sorted. In 2004 she started to look for a place of her own, which needed to be close enough to Ibiza Town to enable her to meet her clients, but also remote enough to be able to get away from it all. She finally discovered a tiny finca nestled in the hills above the town, framed by two tall palm trees.

Serena's finca is small, with only a bedroom, a bathroom and a dressing room, but it has a large covered terrace that overlooks a curved swimming pool. She tends to spend most of her time outdoors on the terrace, which functions as an open-plan kitchen, dining room and living room. To create an extra room, Serena has set up a tipi in the garden. This is her comfortable bedroom, furnished with a double bed, tables and lamps, and a Persian kilim that was a present from a favourite client.

As a keen chef, Serena wanted to have somewhere to entertain friends, and the finca, with its huge terrace, swimming pool and traditional wood-

LEFT, TOP, AND OPPOSITE Serena commissioned her tipi to her own design from 100% Ibiza, near Santa Eulària.

LEFT, BOTTOM Serena's ingenious solution to creating another room: the tipi, with a large double bed between tables and lamps, makes a comfortable bedroom.

fired oven, is perfectly designed for outdoor living. The kitchen and dining area fills one end of the terrace, with a large Spanish wooden table and chairs that she found in the flea market at the Hippodromo (the old race course) in San Jordi. Serena's terracotta plates, bowls and dishes are all from Ibiza. She brought the white lace tablecloth and black-and-white earthenware plates back from her travels in Ecuador. The heart-shaped cups and saucers came from Casa y Campo in Ibiza Town.

Hanging along the roof of the terrace is a string of brightly coloured fairy lights from the hippy market in Las Dalias. A red velvet sofa for lounging on, from Can Rich, has three decorative Japanese paper umbrellas from the party decoration shop in Ibiza Town hanging above it. One of the cult shops in Ibiza is Deseo, on Benirras beach, which sells kaftans, paintings and hand-painted shoes, and Serena picked up her fluoro Buddha paintings here. She tends to collect furniture and accessories from all over Ibiza, mixing new discoveries with market finds. At the edge of the pool, huge fluoro cushions from Sluiz, the hippy shop on the San Josep road, are flung beneath two palm trees, and brightly coloured lanterns, a bargain from her local supermarket Hippocentro, light the pool area.

Serena's home is a real retreat and she loves sitting and looking out over the lights of Ibiza Town when she gets home late at night. When she finally goes to bed, she sleeps under canvas, in the tipi in the garden.

OPPOSITE Serena shops for dresses and kaftans at Las Dalias (the hippy market) and Deseo on Benirras beach.

RIGHT, TOP This is the view from the terrace, which looks out over the swimming pool and the palm trees towards Ibiza Town.

RIGHT, BOTTOM The small stone finca, housing a bedroom and a bathroom, is seen behind the terrace. To the far right is the wood-fired outdoor oven.

OVERLEAF The rustic terrace has walls and columns built from Ibizan stone and a terracotta tiled floor. The wooden Spanish table and chairs and the red velvet sofa combine to make a comfortable living and dining area.

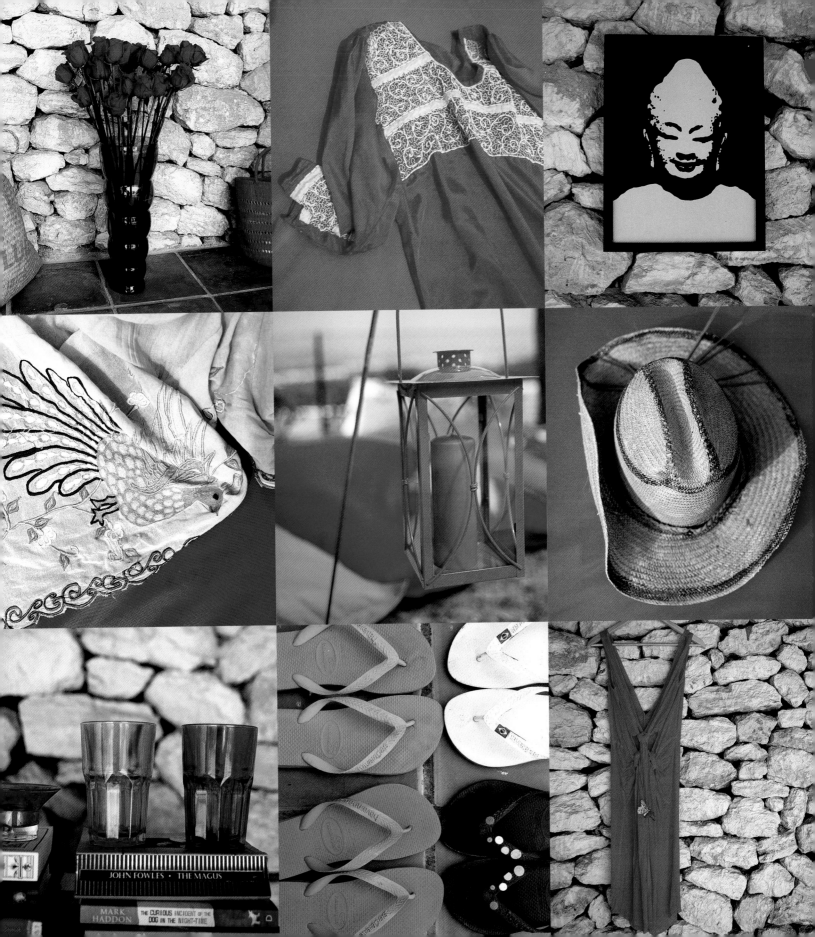

Los Patios

Johnny Bute's parents brought him to Ibiza on holiday in the 1960s and 1970s, when the island was still undeveloped. Thirty years later, inspired by his childhood memories, Johnny wanted to bring his own family here. The location of Los Patios was key to its attraction for Johnny and his wife, Serena: it is not surrounded by any other properties and it backs on to a national park, with steep cliffs and forests.

Los Patios was built by a French architect in the style of a Mexican hacienda. It was built on a grand scale, with high ceilings and wooden beams stretching 5.5 metres (18 feet) across. It can easily accommodate fourteen people in its seven bedrooms, which are scattered throughout the main house and in the pool house. Johnny describes it as a big, rambling family home, and he particularly likes its linear design, with almost all the rooms on the same level. It is perfect for children, as there can be a big noisy scene down at the pool, and no one can hear it at the other end of the house.

The previous owner left the house almost fully furnished, and the Butes have worked with what was left behind, keeping some things and altering others. The once dark kitchen, for example, has been completely transformed, with rendered shelving and limed hardwood units made to measure by an Ibizan builder, but the large white sofas and marble-topped tables came with the house. Serena bought fabric from Ibiza Town to make new cushions and curtains for the kitchen and living room. During the spring and autumn, the family gathers around the open fire in the living room: it is a cosy, sunken den area, with two sofas facing each other, piled with cushions made by Serena.

LEFT, TOP TO BOTTOM, AND OPPOSITE The vivid colour of
Los Patios creates a vibrant Mexican feel, making it quite
unlike any other house on the island.

The main bedroom had a metal-framed bed, which Johnny and Serena liked so much that they decided to have it copied by a local blacksmith for other bedrooms in the house. They have customized their bedroom with such finds from local shops as the Moroccan-inspired ceramic bedside table, the lampshades and the wall hanging. The bathrooms were decorated by a team of Moroccan craftsmen, with vividly coloured tiles applied freehand to create unique designs. They are constantly on the lookout for great furniture and textiles for the house.

Serena and Johnny worked hard to restore the gardens, planting orange trees along the drive, and maintaining the lush green lawn. Johnny has recently bought an adjoining plot of land, which he plans to turn into an orchard filled with fruit trees. They have planted bougainvillea on the terrace, to shade their outdoor dining table, and have hung a mirror on the back wall to reflect the view of the garden. There is also a fully equipped kitchen and dining area by the pool. Cupboards here are filled with brightly coloured Moroccan-inspired ceramic plates, bowls and coffee cups from the local town of San Josep.

During the summer, Johnny swims every morning at the local beach, Cala d'Hort, which faces the towering myth-inspiring rock of Es Vedra. The rest of the family tends to stay by the pool, where a Moroccan tent provides shade and is the perfect place for afternoon siestas. Hammocks hang from the palm trees, while around the swimming pool there are daybeds that are perfect for lounging on after lunch.

OPPOSITE The outdoor spaces give the house a hacienda-like feel. Arched columns keep this room open to the elements beneath a sabina-wood beamed ceiling. The traditional Spanish table and chairs have brightly coloured cushions made by Serena.

RIGHT, TOP A Rajasthani four-poster bed in one of the guest bedrooms is swathed in mosquito netting.

RIGHT, BOTTOM In the cosy sunken seating area the two low sofas, built out from the walls, have red ikat cushions made by Serena. Family photos cover the walls.

Atzaro

When the Guasch family began to question their traditional way of life at the north of the island in their old finca and farming estate, where their family had lived for centuries, a discussion with their friend Philip Gonda prompted their decision to convert the property into a new type of agroturismo hotel. Atzaro was to be a luxurious place to stay amid the farmland and orange groves of the Ibizan countryside.

Philip Gonda had been looking for a project to invest in, and he and the Guasch family worked on the conversion together. There is a total of five houses on the estate. The original farmhouse is thought to be more than 270 years old, and planning laws meant that the ancient walls had to be preserved, with the result that the kitchen walls are more than 1 metre (3 feet) thick. Work began on the hotel in 2001 and progressed quickly, with the kitchen, dining room and guest rooms completed in just eighteen months. Over the next few years, two of the houses were converted into luxurious private villas, linked to the hotel.

As a pilot, Philip travelled all over the world, but he was always drawn back to Asia and Africa. The design concept at Atzaro is an eclectic mix of Ibizan, African and Asian styles. Philip says: "We've got about eleven countries represented here, from Asia to Africa – deep central Africa, South Africa, Sudan, Ethiopia, Morocco, Libya, Tunisia, Java, Bali, Thailand

LEFT, TOP AND BOTTOM The huge palm trees in the Moroccan-inspired garden were imported from Egypt. Intimate seating areas are scattered throughout the grounds and illuminated at night with Moroccan lanterns and candles.

OPPOSITE Stone steps lead up to the traditional white-washed seventeenth-century farmhouse. The new floor-to-ceiling windows reveal the warm, rustic design of the hotel's restaurant.

and the Philippines – but we also have typical Ibizan architecture." He was particularly drawn to a pared-down aesthetic and wanted the villas to have a minimalist, Zen appeal. The Guasch family were simply relieved to breathe new life into their crumbling old property.

Popular with the guests are the rooms decorated in a luxurious but minimalist style, such as the Lavanda suite, with its own private plunge pool, daybeds, fountains and terrace. Most of the guest rooms have a Mediterranean feel, with terracotta-tiled floors, smooth plaster walls and sabina-wood ceilings, while the Asian influence may be see in the wooden doors inlaid with mother-of-pearl, sourced in Timor.

The main house is decorated in a more rustic Ibizan style, with Asian, African and Arabian influences. The dining room at Atzaro has a typically warm feel, decorated in earth tones, with orange and red cushions, and dark wooden Indonesian and Moroccan tables and chairs. To give the restaurant a more contemporary feel, square plates and stainless-steel cutlery designed in mainland Spain were chosen. The restaurant has one of the best menus in Ibiza; wherever possible, fresh local produce is used, including fruit, vegetables and eggs from the Guasch family farm.

OPPOSITE, TOP LEFT A stone sculpture of the Buddha stands on either side of the entrance to one of the spa treatment rooms.

OPPOSITE, TOP RIGHT, AND LEFT, BOTTOM One of the spa treatment rooms, which was carved by hand from Bankirai wood and teak in Java.

OPPOSITE, BOTTOM LEFT The swimming pool at Atzaro is surrounded by old olive and palm trees. Low Moroccan tables and fountains and ponds create cool, shady spaces.

OPPOSITE, BOTTOM RIGHT A detail of the carvings on the façade of the treatment room.

LEFT, TOP In the dining room, contemporary Spanish art hangs on the stone wall and contrasts with the antique Spanish chairs and Balinese tables.

Asian and African influences are particularly visible in the Moroccan-inspired garden, which has eleven fountains and is dotted with huge palm trees imported from Egypt. Throughout the grounds there are 3000 orange trees, which produce fruit twice a year. At Easter-time the air is heady with the scent of orange blossom, and during the summer months the garden is filled with live music or laid-back, chilled-out sounds played by DJs. Along one wall of the garden are large daybeds with canopies, modelled on those of the celebrated chill-out club Ku De Ta in Bali.

Philip did all the landscaping at Atzaro, from the gardens and terraces to the pools and fountains. The long, narrow swimming pool leading up to the spa is one of the most dramatic features: around 40 metres (130 feet) long, it is built from dark-green stone and marble from the Indonesian island of Sulawesi. Philip describes his design concept: "I wanted to give it the feeling of a slow-moving stream, meandering through a thick canopy of trees." The spa was designed to look like Balinese wooden temples, and each of the treatment rooms was hand-built in Java, using Bankirai and teak wood. For accents of colour, Philip picked out lacquered red bamboo from Bali.

Evening at Atzaro is a magical experience, with the air filled with the scent of orange blossom and the fountains and gardens illuminated. Everywhere you look there is somewhere comfortable to sit and relax: daybeds are placed next to the fountains, and tables and chairs beneath the trees. This is the place to sip cocktails, eat tapas and listen to some of the best music in Ibiza. Afterwards you can choose to slip away to a minimalist Zen villa or to one of the rustic farmhouse bedrooms. Atzaro has brought a whole new level of luxury to Ibiza, without losing any of the island's relaxed charm.

LEFT, TOP AND BOTTOM The Asian- and Mediterranean-inspired guest rooms have their own private terraces. Furniture is made from exotic hardwoods in clean, modern shapes, while cushions and textiles in bold colours provide contrast.

contemporary style

KavaKava

After years of regularly holidaying in Ibiza, Céline and Jean-François Nguyen decided to move to the island, from New York, after the terrorist attacks in the US in late 2001, when it "felt like a safe haven". Céline says that they fell in love with the setting of KavaKava: "We liked the location on top of the hill, surrounded by pine forests. It felt very peaceful and very quiet."

The house is an old finca that was converted in the Moroccan style in the 1970s. Making their mark on it has been a slow process for Céline and Jean-François, with changes made little by little. "Year after year," says Céline, "we have knocked down more of the house!" Céline enjoys living in a place for a while before making changes, to get to know "which areas you like and where the sun comes in". The downstairs bedrooms and terrace were finally completed in the spring of 2006.

With the help of her Brazilian friend Roberto Miranda, a master craftsman, Céline managed to redesign the whole house without having to work with an architect. She drew the plans and Roberto brought them to life, directing works when Céline was out of the country. He also made most of the furniture, from the large white coffee table and the dining table in the living room to the white worktop in the kitchen.

Céline and Jean-François wanted to create a structure that would integrate with the surrounding environment and decided to use only local

LEFT, TOP AND BOTTOM The terrace extends out from the living room, and has views of Las Salinas beach and the sea beyond. There are teak daybeds covered with kilims and cushions, a large sofa from Inbize and a Chinese opium table from La Sabama.

OPPOSITE A large wooden daybed, hung with white muslin curtains and piled with Missoni-print cushions, sits at the edge of the swimming pool.

stone. Their first building projects were to create a new entrance patio around an ancient olive tree, and to renovate the guest house, which overlooks the garden. Next, they opened up the house to its surrounding views; the smallness of the finca's original windows made some of the rooms very dark and meant that it was hard to see out into the garden or to the forest beyond. Céline and Jean-François "love being surrounded by nature and wanted to enjoy it from inside the house".

On arriving at KavaKava, the first space a visitor sees is the outdoor terrace, which is a riot of colour, with teak beds draped with bright kilims and peppered with cushions covered in stripes and flowers from the Italian fashion house Missoni. The furniture on the terrace was picked up by Céline from the flea markets in Paris and local shops in Ibiza: the big teak sofas come from Inbize and the Chinese opium table from La Sabama.

Inside traditional Ibizan fincas, seating is built into the walls in the form of curved platforms, which are often covered with cushions. Céline liked the idea of using this concept inside her new interior, and all the seating in the living room has been built in, in the traditional way. She also felt that "it captured something of the lounging spirit of Ibiza: you can lie around where you want, and have the most amazing view outside". All the cushions in the room are covered in suede and velvet from Brazil. There is

OPPOSITE The living room is a modern take on traditional Ibizan design. The low bench seating was built against the wall, and the seats are upholstered in suede and velvet from Brazil. The curved sculpture seen on the right was from Becker in Santa Gertrudis and the fibre-optic lamp hanging on the left was made by Ibizan sculptor Roseline.

RIGHT, TOP The dining-room chairs, with perspex legs and Missoni-print seats, were designed by Philippe Starck and are from Becker in Santa Gertrudis.

RIGHT, BOTTOM The teak furniture on the terrace is given a colourful touch of comfort with Missoni-print cushions and throws.

ABOVE, LEFT A 'Bubble' chair, designed by Eero Aarnio, is softened by a Missoni cushion.

ABOVE, RIGHT To create the outdoor dining area, Céline went to local shops for the furniture, textiles and glassware. The wrought-iron dining table and chairs are from La Sabama, the bright, striped tablecloth from Textura, and the coloured glasses from Pomelo.

a grey crystal lamp that hangs in spirals over the coffee table and was created by Ibizan sculptor Roseline. It is made from fibre optics, which glow in the dark, and is one of Céline's favourite pieces.

Down a few steps from the main living room is a more intimate lounging area, arranged around the original fireplace. A double-height space has been created from what was a small dark room, and huge windows on either side of the fireplace look out on to the pine forest. This is where Céline and Jean-François spend winter evenings, wrapped in an Hermès blanket in front of a roaring fire.

Despite the open-plan scheme of most of the house, Céline and Jean-François wanted to create a separate area just for themselves. Their bedroom and bathroom are essentially one large room, with a huge wooden frame separating the two spaces, like an open window. Céline likes the fact that even when you are in the bathroom, you can take in the amazing view. As she says, "usually bathrooms don't have any view at all".

At the back of the house, wide wooden terraces overlook the swimming pool, inherited as a keyhole shape from the previous owner. Céline did not like the unusual shape, and came up with the ingenious idea of building a rectangle around the original pool and increasing the depth of the water by 20 centimetres (8 inches), to create a ledge around the perimeter where one can sit or lie in shallow water while chatting to friends. Artfully arranged around the pool is a selection of huge white sunbeds, wooden loungers and Indian coffee tables, and a large wooden daybed hung with white muslin curtains. Scattered over all of these are brightly printed Missoni towels and cushions.

KavaKava has a strong individual style that is quite unlike that of many homes in Ibiza, where inspiration tends to be taken from such places as Morocco and Bali. In common with their fellow Ibizan residents, however, Céline and Jean-François are generous hosts, and their unique villa is often filled with friends visiting from around the world.

ABOVE, LEFT With a roaring fire and a view of the mountains, this intimate sitting room is where Céline and Jean-François relax during the chilly winter months.

ABOVE, RIGHT The bedroom has a light and airy feel, with sliding glass doors leading out on to the terrace and windows overlooking the pine forest.

OVERLEAF, LEFT A large teak daybed on one of the terraces is piled with cushions covered in boldly patterned Missoni fabric.

OVERLEAF, RIGHT The bathroom floor is made of IPE exotic wood and the walls are Spanish travertino. The sink and bath are from Palau in Ibiza and the taps are by Hansgrohe.

Can Sebastian

Sebi Properzi, a musician, and his girlfriend, Kika Morini, a contemporary dancer, needed a building or studio that could be used as a live—work space. They found a warehouse-style building close to San Antonio, surrounded by almond trees, and decided to buy the property in 2001.

Can Sebastian was originally an industrial building, but the previous owner, an architect, decided that it could be an interesting place to live and had begun to convert it before Sebi and Kika found it. There was still a great deal of work to be done, though, and Sebi and Kika moved into a bare shell with concrete floors, bringing with them only a futon mattress and the technical equipment for Sebi's studio. Far from being depressed about living in an empty house with no furniture, Sebi and Kika loved the space, which allowed them to appreciate the light flooding in through the huge windows. Being on the west side of the island, their house is ideally positioned for views of the famous Ibizan sunsets.

When they moved into their empty house, Sebi and Kika discovered a necklace hanging on the wall and a painting of a spaceship, which they decided to leave exactly as they had found them. Every evening their home is filled with orange light as the sun sets, and this has formed the basis for the interior colour scheme. As Sebi explains: "The orange colour came from the light on the floor. I thought it just looked right — the

LEFT, TOP AND BOTTOM Surrounded by gardens full of fruit and almond trees, Can Sebastian enjoys a rural setting that contrasts with its urban-looking industrial design.

OPPOSITE From Sebi's mezzanine work studio, most of the open-plan living space can be seen below. The industrial interior of the building reveals its structure of metal beams and galleried supports, reflecting its history as a warehouse.

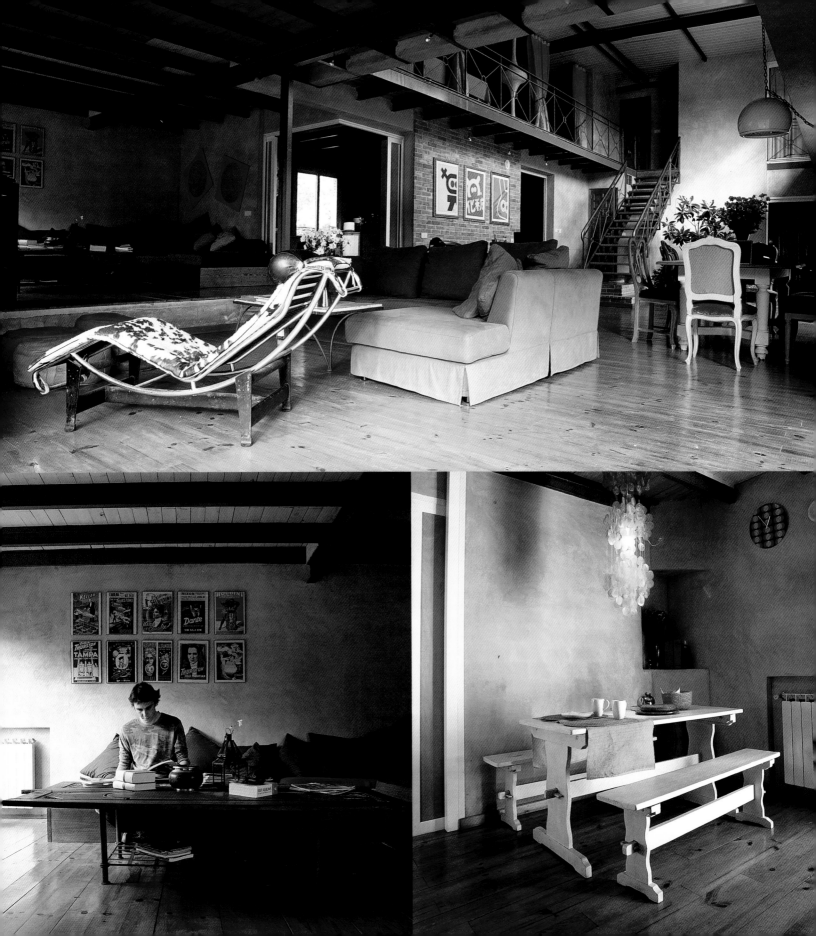

colour is quite warm and the light looks golden, so we thought to buy everything in orange." Sebi and Kika chose a warm wooden floor with an orange glow, and had it installed throughout the house. The windows are covered with bright-orange curtains.

The ground floor is entirely open-plan, with a few steps separating the kitchen, dining and sitting areas. Finding furniture to fit the space was difficult, so Kika and Sebi decided to buy antique and modern pieces and customize them to fit. Around the dining table, the wooden chairs now have jewel-coloured velvet seats, and have been painted in vibrant contrasting colours. Modern posters are presented in second-hand wooden frames, painted gold for an antique look. All the low tables are made from old Balinese doors, picked up in Ibiza. To create an intimate sitting area, the couple built a low, L-shaped daybed in the corner of the room. They covered the daybed with blankets from Marrakech, and made the cushions themselves, from vintage fabrics.

OPPOSITE, TOP The open-plan living room is an eclectic mix of vintage pieces such as the Le Corbusier chaise longue, previously owned by Sebi's grandfather, and new and customized pieces.

OPPOSITE, BOTTOM LEFT Sebi sits on a low daybed behind a coffee table that was made from an old door. Framed posters of American magicians hang on the wall.

OPPOSITE, BOTTOM RIGHT A vintage table and benches create a cosy sitting area in one corner of the kitchen.

LEFT, TOP Sebi and Kika bought wooden dining chairs that they customized with brightly coloured paint and velvet seats. Propped against the wall is Sebi's guitar case, which is covered in stickers from gigs around the world.

LEFT, BOTTOM The low wooden daybed was made by Sebi and Kika. The three prints on the wall behind are by English design agency The Designers Republic.

Favourite pictures hang in the living area, including a collection of early twentieth-century American posters of old magicians, such as Houdini, on display behind the daybeds. The graphic pictures on the walls are by English design agency The Designers Republic. Objects that have escaped customization include two of their favourite vintage pieces: a radio bought at auction in Santa Gertrudis and an old telephone that belonged to Sebi's grandfather.

Sebi's studio occupies the first-floor landing of the house, facing the huge windows hung with orange curtains. The orange sofas were inherited from his grandfather in Tuscany, along with other furniture from the 1970s. The walls are hung with Sebi's favourite paintings, including "canvases made by a graffiti artist in New York, and a painting from a movie about the 1930s painter Mark Gertler".

On a trip to Morocco in 2004 Sebi and Kika discovered the markets in Marrakech, and Kika admits, "we went crazy and wanted to buy everything!" They ended up with lots of blankets and cushions, Moroccan pouffes in four different colours for the living area, and a new bedcover to match the velvet chairs in the bedroom.

Kika and Sebi designed the bedroom together, with Sebi assembling complicated Japanese folding paper lamps and Kika picking out velvet chairs from the flea market in San Jordi and a vintage chest of drawers from Santa Gertrudis. More vintage pieces from Sebi's grandfather include the green bedside tables and lamps. Kika's bags and clothes decorate the bedroom; a blue feather bag from Bali, and dresses and kurtas from Deseo,

RIGHT, TOP This velvet-covered chair in the bedroom came from a flea market in San Jordi.

RIGHT, BOTTOM Sebi and Kika found this inlaid wooden chest-of-drawers for their bedroom in an antique shop in Santa Gertrudis in Ibiza that specializes in pieces from the 1950s. To complement the geometric shapes in the design, Sebi bought a contemporary Japanese lamp and twisted it into shape.

a shop on Benirras beach, hang on the walls. Kika used to spend winters in India, and she once brought back a beautiful jewellery box, now displayed in front of the bathroom mirror and full of treasures picked up on her travels to India and South Africa – along with "antique brooches and fake jewellery from Accessorize and Top Shop". Kika also picked out coloured towels, a lilac basket from Bali and a woven Ibizan basket for the bathroom.

When Sebi and Kika first moved in, everything in the house had to be coloured, even the towels and sheets, but now they sometimes find themselves yearning for a clean, white space instead of big, bold colours. It will be interesting to see what happens: whether the house becomes a blank white canvas, or even more vibrant and colourful after another trip to Morocco.

OPPOSITE The brick walls of the guest room are softened with taffeta curtains and a bright-pink throw on the bed. A zebra-print chaise longue at the foot of the bed creates a bold contrast.

ABOVE, LEFT The pouffes of various colours that are dotted about the living area came from Morocco.

ABOVE, RIGHT A lamp made of shells, designed by Verner Panton, hangs above the dining table.

La Ventana

Native Ibizan Pepita Ferrer has owned hotels in Ibiza Town for more than thirty years. During this time, she says, everything has changed – including Ibizans themselves, who have learned to adapt to the many new arrivals. Pepita feels that the influx of tourists and travellers has been a positive thing for the island, and she loves the melting pot of cultures that Ibiza Town has become: "There are so many crazy people living here – people love to come and look at the hippies, artists and eccentrics!"

Pepita bought La Ventana in 2006, and, after a brief period of refurbishment, the hotel opened for the summer of that year. The interiors of the hotel were designed by Francesca Moseby, to be a haven of peace and calm amid the bustling streets of the old town. La Ventana is an eighteenth-century townhouse, overlooking the ancient town walls, cobbled streets and garden squares. Francesca transformed it into an intimate boutique hotel, with thirteen bedrooms, a roof terrace and a bijou restaurant.

Harlequin paintings by local artist Grillo Demo hang in the entrance hall, above velvet-covered button-down sofas and armchairs. From here, steps lead through to the cosy, yellow-painted dining room. Linen-covered tables and chairs create a contemporary feel, in contrast to the Spanish antiques, ornate gilt candelabras and large oil paintings.

Opening on to balconies that overlook garden squares and bougainvillea-clad city walls, and with wooden-beamed ceilings

LEFT, TOP AND BOTTOM The old heart of Ibiza Town features the fourteenth-century cathedral of Our Lady of the Snows and cobbled streets lined with buildings that date back to the reign of King Felippe II of Spain in the sixteenth century.

OPPOSITE At the front of the hotel the tall French windows, with traditional shutters, open on to elegant balconies.

and painted shutters, the bedrooms are some of the most romantic in Ibiza. Four-poster beds, made from wrought iron in the Spanish style, are swathed in linen curtains or draped with mosquito netting. The walls are painted a cool blue and the doors and skirting-boards a pale yellow, to create a soothing atmosphere. Each room has an individual feel. Vintage lamps and Spanish antiques mixed with contemporary art create a unique look.

Decorated in La Ventana's signature cool blue and yellow, a winding staircase has been installed to unify the house, linking the bedrooms on each floor, and leading up to a roof terrace with panoramic views. A huge glass lantern, more than 1 metre (3 feet) long, is suspended from the ceiling to illuminate the staircase. The roof terrace is at the very top of the hotel, sheltered by a tent-like Moroccan awning, with benches built into the surrounding walls. Moroccan tables, terracotta pots filled with flowers, and benches piled with cushions add to the relaxed feel. Guests come up here to unwind, lounging on cushions, sipping mint tea and gazing over the terracotta roofs of Ibiza Town.

Tables outside on the cobblestones are the only indicator that this is a hotel rather than a private house. This is the perfect place for watching the life of Ibiza Town go by, as you sip a leisurely morning coffee or enjoy evening cocktails by candle-light.

OPPOSITE, TOP LEFT The entrance hall has a traditional pebbled floor and a wood-burning stove for warmth on winter evenings.

OPPOSITE, BOTTOM LEFT The intimate dining room is painted a vibrant yellow, with contemporary linen-covered chairs, antique oil paintings and gilt-framed mirrors.

OPPOSITE, TOP AND BOTTOM RIGHT A spiral staircase runs through the building and is illuminated by a dramatic Moroccan lantern.

OVERLEAF, LEFT One of the romantic bedrooms at La Ventana has a wrought-iron four-poster bed hung with linen curtains, in the Spanish style.

OVERLEAF, RIGHT The same colour scheme is followed throughout the hotel, with decorative details adding touches of luxury.

Can Truy Covas

Chico and Linde Bialas have a living and working partnership that dates back more than forty years. Chico, a celebrated fashion photographer, worked in Paris during the supermodel era of the 1980s and 1990s, with Linde as his art director. Having enjoyed a holiday home on the island for more than thirty years, the couple decided to leave Paris and make their home in Ibiza in 1996. Linde has been painting since they moved to Can Truy Covas and has had a number of sell-out exhibitions of her work, much of which draws inspiration from life in Ibiza.

When Chico and Linde discovered an old finca near Santa Agnes, it seemed like the perfect project, having extensive grounds, and outbuildings that could be converted into studios. They wanted to create a very natural, unpretentious environment. Chico explains that in the garden they "wanted to use only plants that grew here and not strange stuff from other places. It still looks like an old Ibizan landscape." Even the swimming pool, rather than being the usual blue rectangle, is an Ibizan water reservoir, chosen to blend in with its surroundings.

A rugged dirt road leads up to the front door, and on the other side of the house a narrow grassy track runs into the garden, following the contour of the hillside. This track, or *camino*, is thought to be hundreds of years old, and is the way the original inhabitants would have driven

LEFT, TOP AND BOTTOM Exterior walls of the old finca have been left as they were found, including a painted white cross that, according to Ibizan tradition, wards off evil spirits.

OPPOSITE The ancient grassy *camino* and dry-stone walls lead to the kitchen door of the old finca.

OPPOSITE This intimate sitting room has a wire table and chairs from a flea market in Paris placed on a rug from Uzbekistan. Traditional Ibizan seating has been built against the wall.

LEFT, TOP Design classics in the living room include a 1940s lamp and a glass table by Mies van der Rohe. A painting by Linde fills the end wall of the living room.

LEFT, BOTTOM This view of the dining room shows the French table surrounded by Taulec chairs. One of Linde's paintings from 2005 hangs on the wall.

OVERLEAF, TOP LEFT The walls of Chico and Linde's bedroom are hung with paintings by David Hockney, Richard Hamilton, Jim Dine and Linde herself. The bed has a simple white cover from Zara Home. The table beside it was designed by Chico, the lamp was from Artemide and the chair is African and from a Parisian collector.

OVERLEAF, TOP RIGHT AND BOTTOM LEFT An installation by Martin Bialas is seen on the library wall.

OVERLEAF, BOTTOM RIGHT The cement reservoir is less obtrusive than a conventional modern swimming pool would be. The plants in the garden are all indigenous to the island.

OVERLEAF, FAR RIGHT Linde's studio is in one of the outbuildings. Recent figurative works on canvas and paper can be seen on the walls and floor, while Linde prepares for an exhibition in the south of France.

their carts up to the finca. Local influences can be seen throughout the house, from the walls painted with a limewash solution made from local chalk to the old Ibizan tiles used for the kitchen worktop. These antique tiles were traditionally used on the front steps of Ibizan town houses.

Throughout their years in Paris, Chico and Linde regularly went to their local flea market, where they would pick up naïve, quirky paintings that caught their eye. Some of these are now on display on the kitchen wall, next to a Moroccan sign that reads "Room for Rent". Chico's favourite black-and-white pictures of their children and grandchildren are pinned to the noticeboard. The old terracotta floor-tiles are from the south of France, as are the vintage chairs, which were bought in Arles.

Flea-market finds also include a metal table and chairs in the small living room, and an antique chandelier and mirror in the guest bathroom. One of Chico and Linde's favourite antique shops in Paris specialized in 1940s industrial metal lamps, and some of these are now used as free-standing reading lights in the living room and library. Roughly woven antique rugs from Morocco and Uzbekistan lend colour to the polished-concrete floors.

The huge white walls of the finca make the perfect backdrop for installation sculptures by Chico and Linde's son, Martin, and his work can be seen throughout the living room, library and study, alongside Linde's paintings of bold, confident women. One of Linde's most recent paintings, from 2005, hangs in the dining room, above an antique French country table that is surrounded by burnished-steel Taulec chairs from Paris.

OPPOSITE AND RIGHT, TOP TO BOTTOM Linde's studio is in one of the outbuildings, where examples of her recent figurative works on canvas and paper line the walls.

Antique glass Lauterne lamps from the Saint-Sulpice market in Paris hang from the ceiling, and contrast dramatically with the white paper lamps by Noguchi.

Light pours into the living room from a rooftop skylight, illuminating Linde's painting on the far wall. One of Martin's installation sculptures provides an elegant contrast on the adjoining wall. This room is filled with classic design pieces, including a Charles Eames leather armchair and footstool and a glass table by Mies van der Rohe.

Set apart from the main building is Chico's study, which used to be a farm outbuilding and still contains the old stone olive press. Smoke from an old outdoor oven had blackened one inside wall, but Chico loved the effect and the wall has been left as it was found. He has hung his favourite pictures in the studio: a huge figurative painting of a woman upside down, painted by Linde in 1996, and one of his own poster-sized black-and-white prints of Italian actress Monica Bellucci.

Making the move from Paris to Ibiza has revitalized the work of both Chico and Linde and introduced them to a new group of cosmopolitan friends. Living on the island has given them both a new source of inspiration, and together they have produced a series of photographs and paintings reflecting their life here.

LEFT, TOP The kitchen table stands on the old terracotta-tiled floor. A collection of vintage jugs and vases is displayed on the shelving behind.

LEFT, BOTTOM A terracotta urn, with its painted surface almost completely peeled away, reflects the emphasis on texture that charaterizes Chico and Linde's choice of furnishings.

vintage inspiration

Can Canel

Italian marchesa Alessandra Castelbarco was inspired to look for a home in Ibiza by a desire for a more bohemian, less restricted way of life than she had found in Italy. She moved to the island in the 1990s and settled there with her son, her boyfriend and their daughter, believing it to be a good place to raise her family.

Ale, as she prefers to be called, had a specific idea of what she wanted, and had to look for four years to find the right property: "I wanted a big house and I wanted to make my house out of an old one, so it was not so easy." When she first went to view what would become her home, the agent did not have the keys but put pressure on her to decide whether or not to buy it because another client was interested. She ran round trying to look in through the windows, and now recalls: "The important thing for me was to see the sabina-wood beams, because normally when you see a house with this kind of roof, it means that it's old." Although it was nerve-racking to do so, Ale made up her mind to buy the finca on the spot.

Thought to be around four hundred years old, Ale's finca originally would have had one central living space with a fireplace in the corner. Smaller rooms leading off this space were used for storing grain and stabling animals, and the outdoor terraces would have been used for

OPPOSITE In the depths of the countryside, this ancient finca, with its open-air terraces and tiny windows, has remained virtually unchanged since the seventeenth century.

ABOVE, LEFT The old stone staircase leads to the upstairs bedroom and terrace. The rocking-horse and grandfather clock are antiques inherited from Ale's family.

ABOVE, RIGHT This view of Ale's bedroom shows the wide wooden floorboards, the Indian velvet bedcovers, and the sabina-beamed ceiling characteristic of Ibizan fincas.

drying figs and almonds. The most recent owners had divided the building into two homes and Ale was keen to turn it back into one big house, so she took out the division. It took three years, and Ale lived in the stables while the conversion was going on; or, as she put it, "I was really living inside the refurbishment".

At one end of the house Ale built a new kitchen and at the other she created new bedrooms for herself and her son, Blu. She knocked through the walls of four small rooms to create two further bedrooms. Working on her own, Ale admits that she made mistakes: "I always knew that I wanted many kids but for some reason there is only one bedroom close to mine – all the others are spread around the house."

There are many original features still in the finca: the upstairs bedroom, for example, still has the original tiled floor. But what looks like an old farm kitchen, on the other hand, is actually brand new, being a show kitchen that Ale fell in love with when she went to buy tiles for the house.

One of Ale's friends helped her build the new bathrooms. On the walls they used a traditional technique called *marmolina*, in which powdered marble is mixed with coloured pigment to give a result like polished plaster. One bathroom is a vivid green and the other is bright blue. Ale says, "my son is called Blu and so everything I choose for him is strictly blue".

On the terrace, Blu's old wooden bed has been transformed into a lounge bed, with cushions and throws made from fabric that Ale brought back from India. The lanterns are from Bali, while the Moroccan cushions and throws are from Ale's favourite second-hand shop in Ibiza, Can Castillo: "It's a typical place where they go around Spain and collect all the things to sell. It's a small place and you can find interesting pieces." The wrought-iron candlesticks were made by Blu's father.

The comfortable living room incorporates tall wooden bookshelves, warm rugs on the floor and sofas arranged in an L-shape in the corner. Ale picked up the sofas and lamps from a second-hand shop in Ibiza. With her

ABOVE, LEFT Ale built two large wooden bookcases in the living room, to house her collection of books. In front of them are two reading chairs and an antique rug from Ale's father.

ABOVE, RIGHT The huge L-shaped sofa came from a second-hand shop in Ibiza and forms an intimate seating area in the living room. The terracotta-tiled floor is covered with an antique rug, on top of which is placed a Moroccan pouffe and a vintage Indian table.

boyfriend, she customized the chandelier with crystals. The puppets on the shelf are from a shop in Ibiza Town: "Every year they make a different puppet and I always buy one, and so I love them." The rugs are from her father and the huge painting is by a close Italian friend. All the antique furniture belonged to her mother. The only aspect of the living room that Ale dislikes is the television. She shares the house with her English boyfriend, Brad, and has to compromise about certain things. "I hate television," she says, "but my boyfriend likes it and says it is a very typical English thing!"

Despite the freedom of life in Ibiza, Ale remains focused on building a large and comfortable home for her family and friends. Even though she has left the traditions of Italian life behind, this generosity of spirit and the importance of family continues.

RIGHT, TOP The traditional sabina-wood beams and narrow doorway of the bathroom contrast with Ale's hippy-chic style of decoration, with colourful beads and sunflowers against the bright-green bath and walls made from *marmolina*.

RIGHT, BOTTOM This very feminine bedroom has a vintage French bed furnished with a fluffy pink cover and deep-pink cushions.

Casa Corazon

A former model and actress, Valerie Smith first lived in Ibiza in the 1970s, with her two young children, in a cottage with no running water or electricity. After an absence of nearly twenty years, she returned to the island in 2003, when a friend told her about an old finca in the countryside. The home she has created from the property is a far cry from the derelict farmhouse of her previous life in Ibiza, but it embodies the simplicity of lifestyle that had always been important to Valerie. She worked hard to rebuild the finca and surrounding *corralles* (stables), and now runs her home as a successful small guest house.

In her own living area, Valerie made the kitchen as cosy as possible, putting, for example, a wooden rocking chair in front of a traditional fireplace and painting the surrounding wall a warm, deep red. The adjoining room is a living and dining room, which is decorated in the same striking style and has a wing-backed two-seat sofa covered in leopard-print fabric, a dark-wood Spanish table and a large metal candelabrum.

A major project was to convert the two dilapidated *corralles*, which had no floors or ceilings, into two further guest rooms. Working with her builder, Valerie patiently restored the rooms using local stone, plastering the walls and colouring them with natural earth tones, echoing the same

LEFT, TOP Lavender beds line the terrace surrounding the swimming pool, and a large lemon tree provides an area of much-needed shade.

LEFT, BOTTOM Lloyd Loom chairs complement a vintage wooden table on the terrace of the Sunset Suite. No other houses can be seen from this peaceful terrace, only the quiet valley below.

OPPOSITE This archway links the old finca of Casa Corazon to the new accommodation in the former *corralles*.

warm colour in the terracotta floor. She valued the builder's work as that of a true craftsman: "He chose the most beautiful stones to leave showing through the plaster. He also found all the ancient sabina wood." One of these rooms has its own courtyard with an old fig tree, and the other has a large stone terrace overlooking the valley, with views towards Ibiza Town.

Most of Valerie's conversion budget was spent on new beds and bathrooms for the guest rooms. Each room has a huge bathroom, like a salon, as Valerie loves the idea of being able to chat while having a bath or getting ready to go out. To create a distinctive look, she has introduced vintage English pieces from her own home, together with market finds from Ibiza and antique Spanish furniture. One of the *corralles* has a New Mexican feel, with vintage pareos flung over the beds and a star-shaped table topped with a green-and-white mosaic. The family suite in the main finca building, in contrast, is furnished with hand-stitched English quilts and vintage French linen sheets.

The interiors of the guest rooms change every year. Valerie sees Casa Corazon as a form of artistic expression: "I don't like to have the rooms looking the same; I want to keep rearranging them and having a different look." She says of her own taste: "I think it is quite unique and I haven't really seen many other houses on the island that have this style."

Valerie chose the traditional blue-and-white colour scheme for the outside of the house. An interior courtyard has been treated like an outdoor living room, with tables, chairs and paintings that continue the blue-and-white theme. Against the white walls are two ethereal white

OPPOSITE AND RIGHT, TOP AND BOTTOM Valerie's idiosyncratic style mixes a wing-backed leopard-print sofa with a boldy patterned kilim and velvet cushions. Antique carpets and a Moroccan table enrich the terracotta-tiled floor, and interesting vases, all in shades of blue, fill the windowsill.

paintings by English artist and Ibiza resident Lance Tilbury. In one corner there is an antique round wooden table surrounded by white Lloyd Loom chairs and corner bench seating, piled with blue-and-white cushions. At the end of the terrace is a low white daybed, which is one of Valerie's favourite places for a siesta.

When Valerie first arrived, the finca was completely surrounded by fields and fruit trees, so she had to design the gardens from scratch. She created flowerbeds against the house, filling them with tropical flowers and aloe vera, which contrast with the cool blue-and-white design of the building. Small plants and cuttings fill the terracotta pots displayed around the house. Valerie also designed the small swimming pool. She wanted to make sure it blended into the landscape so she enclosed it with a low stone wall and surrounded this with lavender beds.

At Casa Corazon Valerie has recreated the simplicity of design and relaxed way of life that first drew her to Ibiza, and now her guests can enjoy this idyllic, remote finca and its beautiful surroundings.

RIGHT, BOTTOM Double wooden doors open into the living room, which has such traditional features as sabina-wood beams, built-in seating and a fireplace. Antique mirrors and rugs soften the feel of the room.

OPPOSITE, TOP LEFT One of the new bedrooms in the *corralles*, which has a Mexican theme. A vintage pareo is flung over the daybed. The old stone is visible through the plastering on the walls, and in the ceiling the sabina-wood beams are exposed.

OPPOSITE, BOTTOM RIGHT In one of the *corralles* the large bathroom has a fresh, clean feel, with painted white wicker furniture and cupboards.

Casa Favorita

Grillo Demo left his native Argentina in 1978 to begin a new life in Ibiza as an artist. Today his pictures — most famously his paintings of falling jasmine — are exhibited around the world. His home on the island is a small two-bedroom cottage in the countryside, where he can focus on his work and tend his beloved garden, filled with fragrant honeysuckle and rose trees, and every type of jasmine.

On arriving at the simple white cottage with small blue-framed windows, your eye is drawn to a bright-red swathe of canvas hung next to the front door: a painting of a falling jasmine flower. This dramatic opener prepares you for the riot of colour within. The front door leads into the living room, which is dominated by a large daybed covered in blue-and-coral bed linen designed by Olatz Schnabel. In the kitchen, Grillo exclaims, "Naples yellow, coral and turquoise are the best colours for a house in the sun", and he has painted the doors and window frames in all these colours. The bathroom is painted in a cool eau-de-nil.

Some colours in the house derive from Grillo's travels. In the winter, he leaves Ibiza to travel home to Argentina or to explore other countries. His bedroom is full of finds from India, such as the blue-and-white

LEFT, TOP The cottage seen from a distance across the surrounding fields of wild flowers, and olive, lemon and almond trees.

LEFT, BOTTOM The pergola covered in roses makes a tunnel leading to the door of the cottage. At the other end is a seating area with daybeds and large cushions.

OPPOSITE Beside the front door of the cottage is a striking red painting of a falling jasmine flower, the trademark iconography of Grillo's work.

patchwork quilt and the red nineteenth-century carpet with embroidered gold edging. The mosquito net hanging from the ceiling, on the other hand, is from South America, and the yellow canvas behind the bed was inspired by Tibetan flags. The vivid red used for curtains, cushions and in paintings was also inspired by India. "Colours just come to me and then I put them on," says Grillo, who treats his house as a continually changing artwork.

One of Grillo's closest friends in Ibiza is Vincente Hernandez, the owner of the shop Ganesha in Ibiza Town, which specializes in vintage furniture and antiques. The 1960s lamp in the kitchen and the crucifix hanging behind the bed were both chosen by Vincente for Grillo's house. Fellow artist Julian Schnabel painted Grillo's portrait in Miami on a selection of broken plates and this portrait now has pride of place in his bedroom. Schnabel's wife, Olatz, has covered many of the cushions that are scattered through the house, as well as the bed linen.

Grillo has used his early interest in architecture to create innovative spaces and installations inside the cottage and outside, in the surrounding gardens. In the summer, he makes 'outdoor rooms', with piles of books,

OPPOSITE Grillo draws inspiration for his works from a wide range of sources: this selection includes images of Ganesha from Goa, portraits of Eva Peron from Argentina and some Catholic religious imagery. He cultivates old varieties of roses for their highly perfumed fragrance.

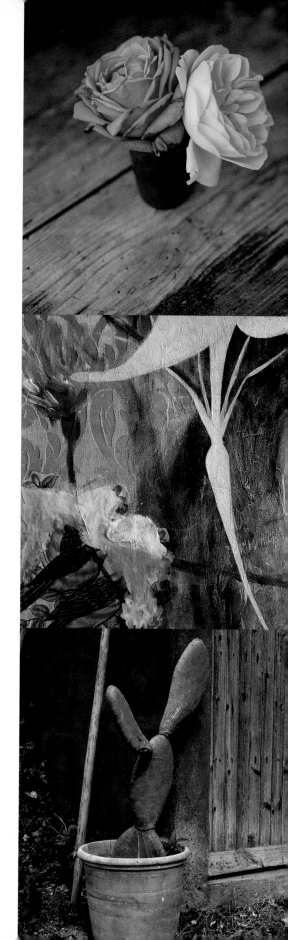

candles, daybeds and cushions under canopies of trailing roses, jasmine and bougainvillea. One particular artwork was created over the summer of 2004, with Grillo forming a towering sculpture from candles and broken objects, until it evolved into an installation for the garden. Placed on a green trestle table by a terracotta wall of trailing roses, it now forms part of an intimate seating area, with turquoise chairs from a charity shop. In front of a pergola of roses, Grillo has placed a daybed next to a low table made from an old Ibizan door. Two eyes, fringed with green and red, look out from a ceramic jug on a rough wooden table. Next to the front door is an African-inspired wooden stool that Grillo made himself.

Grillo constantly changes his home, adding new artworks and finds from his travels, so that, much more than a simple "accumulation of things", it is a fluid and evolving space.

LEFT, TOP The kitchen door and window frames are painted Naples yellow, coral and turquoise. A 1960s lamp from Ganesha hangs above the wooden kitchen table and chairs.

LEFT, BOTTOM A terracotta bust of the goddess Tanit is framed by a painting of falling jasmine and surrounded by candles.

OPPOSITE For the bed, Grillo has mixed contemporary textiles by Olatz Schnabel with a blue-and-white Indian patchwork quilt. Drawings and paintings are scattered across a red nineteenth-century carpet.

Es Pouas

On a quiet hillside in the north-west of Ibiza, textile designer Victoria Durrer-Gasse has made her home in a restored finca. Surrounded by fragrant pine, olive and almond trees, the house is reached by a steep, pot-holed dirt track. Victoria fell in love with this old finca on discovering it in 1997, and together with her husband, François, she spent two years restoring it in traditional Spanish style.

The previous owners had been reluctant to sell the property, as most prospective buyers wanted to tear down the walls and put in big windows, which the owners felt was an inappropriate and distressing thing to do to a building dating back to 1660. Victoria and François were the only potential purchasers who showed themselves to be in tune with the architecture and interested in preserving the character of the finca. Rather than pursuing the clean lines of Balinese architecture or following a Moroccan style – the current trends in Ibiza – Victoria and François wanted to keep their Ibizan finca as it was, with the thick walls and small windows that kept it cool during the summer months.

Inside, the couple's passion for authentic restoration can be seen in the ceiling of the double-height entrance hall, which has been insulated in the traditional way, with plaster mixed with seaweed, paper or newspaper applied between the wooden beams. It can still be seen that all the wood for the ceiling was cut by hand with an axe, with the long

OPPOSITE Es Pouas is surrounded by working farms in the valley of Santa Agnes. This ancient finca has been carefully preserved throughout its four-hundred-year history.

vertical pieces made from sabina wood and the crossbeams made from olive wood. The original stones on the floors are from the quarries in San Matteo, which closed many years ago. Steps lead down from the hall into a guest bedroom, a converted storeroom. The bed is built of stone, extending from the wall, and covered in Victoria's characteristic choice of vibrantly coloured textiles, picked up on her travels in India and Bhutan.

When Victoria and François wanted to restore the ceilings in the kitchen and bathroom, they were lucky enough to pick up some old sabina wood from a finca that was being converted. To rebuild the bathroom walls, they found a Moroccan building specialist who used an ancient polished-plaster technique that involves mixing olive oil and whitewash with cement, which can then be stained any colour.

François and Victoria have made one concession to modernity, installing skylight windows in some of the ceilings: as Victoria admits, the old fincas can be a bit dark. When they built the new kitchen roof, using reclaimed, hand-cut wood, for example, they added a skylight to brighten the room. Victoria describes the kitchen as "a bit of India, jumble sale

OPPOSITE The solid stone staircase leads up to François and Victoria's bedroom and bathroom. The door on the ground floor leads through to the guest bedroom.

RIGHT, TOP AND BOTTOM Variously textured and patterned fabrics in bold colours are used throughout the house.

OVERLEAF, TOP LEFT A Rajasthani tea bed, made of wide wooden planks, is used as a table that dominates the living room, and the low seating built out from the walls is covered in cushions made from antique Uzbekistani fabric.

OVERLEAF, TOP RIGHT The low daybeds, vintage cushions and rush matting make a relaxing spot on the terrace from which to enjoy the view of the valley below.

OVERLEAF, BOTTOM LEFT AND RIGHT The intense Ibizan sunlight is allowed to pour into the traditional finca, whether through an open window or through the new skylight in the entrance hall.

OVERLEAF, FAR RIGHT Victoria brought the riding boots back from Tarifa and Andalucia in southern Spain.

antiques, Ibizan terracotta and baskets". African bowls and sculptures are offset by her vibrantly coloured candlesticks. Hanging from the ceiling is a 1930s chandelier, customized by Victoria and a friend with translucent, brightly coloured glass paint. Beneath the light is a handmade table, commissioned from British designer Tim Jasper. Home-grown oranges sit in a handmade basket on the table.

The whole house is filled with a mix of African sculptures, Nepalese carvings, local Ibizan pottery and finds from London's Portobello Market. François, a doctor for Unicef, brings back unusual bowls, carvings and sculptures from his travels in Africa and Afghanistan. Victoria likes to mix contemporary pieces – for example, a Piers Jackson bird painting – with their African sculptures. In the living room, low sofas are placed on either side of a Rajasthani tea bed that once belonged to a maharaja. François and Victoria also collect antique textiles from Uzbekistan, India, Bali and Indonesia, and Victoria uses them to create unusual cushions and throws.

The first-floor terrace, once used for drying tomatoes and figs, is now one of François and Victoria's favourite spots in which to spend evenings outside, lying on rugs and cushions, and taking in the view of the valley below. They love the view from here, being surrounded by "fincas and old working farms, with sheep and pigs in fields of almond trees".

Life in Ibiza for François, Victoria and their young son, Emile, is about discovering the unspoilt and remote parts of the island. In San Antonio they keep a fishing boat, which they use to explore the hidden coves along the north-west coast. Often they are lucky enough to see dolphins, and there is always another secret deserted cove to discover.

OPPOSITE Beneath the heavy roof-beams, the traditional built-in bed is covered with a bedspread from India and cushions made by Victoria with fabric from Bhutan.

RIGHT, TOP A Moroccan building specialist used an old polished-plaster technique to create the bathroom sink and bath. The beams and shutters were reclaimed from another old finca.

RIGHT, CENTRE AND BOTTOM Soft furnishings around the house reflect Victoria's eclectic taste.

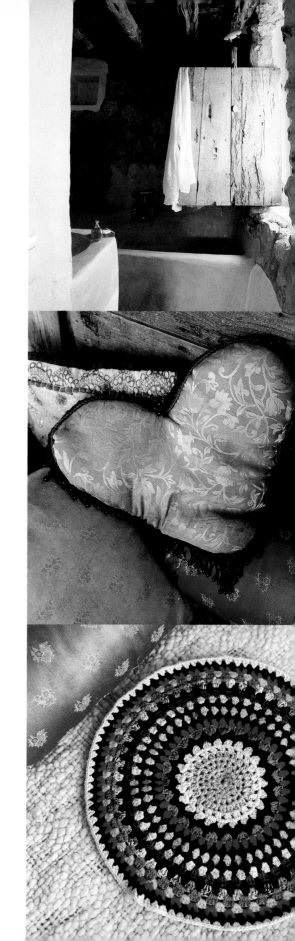

Apartment La Marina

Vincente Hernandez first came to Ibiza more than thirty years ago, arriving early in the morning by boat from Barcelona. "I've been in love since I first saw the colours and light of the island," he says. Originally from Alicante but constantly travelling, he wanted Ibiza to be the place to which he would always return. He has a particular love of the Mediterranean ambience, and his exuberant sense of style has made him an icon of the island.

La Marina is the old neighbourhood surrounding the port in Ibiza Town, full of whitewashed buildings and narrow cobbled streets dating back to the sixeenth century. Vincente owns two boutiques here, one specializing in handmade and vintage clothes and the other in vintage homeware, and both called Ganesha. He had lived in the town for years before managing to acquire the apartment above one of his shops in 2005. Previously owned by four Ibizans, it was a small space divided into four rooms. The first thing Vincente did was to knock down all the internal

OPPOSITE View of the old quarter of Ibiza Town, including the cathedral of Our Lady of the Snows.

RIGHT, TOP Vincente placed a kitsch 1960s-inspired sculpture outside on the terrace.

RIGHT, BOTTOM The white, round dining table by Eero Saarinen, surrounded by white retro chairs from Knoll, creates an intimate dining area. The clear acrylic 'Bubble' chair (just glimpsed) is by Eero Aarnio.

OVERLEAF, LEFT An armchair designed by Pierre Paulin in the 1950s stands in front of the rosewood cabinet that holds many of Vincente's treasures, including drawings by Cocteau and Modigliani.

OVERLEAF, RIGHT In the 1950s-inspired kitchen a vintage glass display stand holds Vincente's collection of jugs, bowls and utensils from the 1960s. On top of the units are Indian sculptures of the Hindu god Ganesha.

walls to create a single open-plan space, with windows on three sides. He installed a 1950s-style kitchen, with a chrome cooker and a Smeg fridge, and a compact bathroom. His bed is shielded behind a screen in one corner of the room, and the rest of the space is divided into separate dining and seating areas. All the furniture in the apartment is vintage, picked up at local markets or found in the street. It is a compact space, but the large French windows, which open on to a balcony swathed in bougainvillea, make the apartment light and airy.

Vincente worked in the fashion industry for years before setting up Ganesha, and he now sells clothes made to his design in India, and rare vintage pieces to such clients as Kate Moss, Jade Jagger and Elle Macpherson. Some customers are invited into his apartment to view new artworks and furniture, and for this reason nothing seems to stay there for more than a few months. His philosophy is that "you become younger by introducing new things to your home". The few pieces that he hangs on to have huge sentimental value: his collection of paintings by the artist Grillo Demo, a series of 'Love' prints by Yves Saint Laurent and an icon of St Peter that belonged to his uncle. On a low bedside table by Knoll sits a picture of Santa Rita, a particularly beloved saint because "she is patron of impossible things and so makes everything OK."

Vincente has a particular love of curvy modern design from the 1960s and 1970s, and has a clear acrylic 'Bubble' chair by Eero Aarnio that hangs in the centre of the room. On the far wall is a long rosewood cabinet on which Vincente has displayed his Yves Saint Laurent 'Love' pictures and two vintage screens, one Art Nouveau and one from the 1950s, which he found "in a dustbin in Ibiza!". In his casual style, he has arranged drawings by Cocteau on top of the cabinet next to pictures by Grillo and one by Modigliani. A photograph of Vincente himself, looking young, lean and tanned, is also propped against the wall, and is signed by Mario Testino. In front of the cabinet are two elegant 1950s armchairs by Pierre Paulin.

Vincente's apartment entirely reflects his unique eye for collecting. His quirky mix of Indian kaftans, vintage fashion and retro design pieces has played a leading role in the creation of the boho-chic Ibizan style.

Les Terrasses

After a period of working in fashion and interior design in Paris, Françoise Pialoux decided to move into the hotel business, following in her grandparents' footsteps. She discovered Les Terrasses in Ibiza by chance, and a neighbour showed her around. It was a simple finca with its own well and some land, although there was no plumbing or electricity. For four years, Françoise worked hard restoring the property, and opened it as a small boutique hotel in 1996.

In order to restore Les Terrasses in a typical Ibizan style, Françoise used as her reference the original fincas, which were traditionally empty and bare. She is keen to make the point that she was not deliberately trying to create a minimalist style, but rather that "the original Ibiza look was copied by the minimalists". She chose a blue-and-white theme for the exterior of Les Terrasses, following a traditional Mediterranean

LEFT, TOP AND BOTTOM Les Terrasses is surrounded by lush gardens. In the summer months, guests take meals outside on the terrace, sitting on canvas director's chairs around painted wooden tables. The finca is painted in the traditional blue and white colours of the Mediterranean.

OPPOSITE Paths wind through the gardens, between the flowers and fruit trees, leading to the guest rooms in the old *corralles*.

ABOVE, LEFT AND RIGHT The extensive grounds have many private seating areas and there is a choice of two swimming pools, one of which is in a secluded area, surrounded by dry-stone walls.

colour scheme, which is also practical, as blue repels insects. Banks of lavender pick up on this soft blue colour scheme.

The guest rooms, created from the various outbuildings, are reached by a labyrinth of patios, stone steps and terracotta paths that lead through the gardens. When Françoise first arrived, there was no garden to speak of, just two lemon trees and a few geraniums. Over the years she has planted palms, olives and cacti, and lots of fruit trees, including lemons, oranges and figs. The garden now provides all the herbs for the hotel restaurant, as well as many of the vegetables. One of Françoise's greatest pleasures is to watch the garden she has created as it changes with the seasons.

Françoise chose not to work with an architect, and took on the conversion of one building at a time herself. Her initial project was to rearrange the main house to create four new bedrooms, and to install a new kitchen and dining room. At a later stage, she converted the *corralles* into bedrooms, making two rooms from each, until there were another

six bedrooms. Each room has its own unique character: the simple white bedroom has a painted wooden floor and a handmade white bedcover, while the pink bedroom has a more feminine feel, with antique white chairs, pink fabric lampshades and an embroidered bedcover. The bathrooms are modern and luxurious, with Philippe Starck fittings and deep tubs for soaking in, or double showers finished with handmade ceramic tiles.

Unlike the guest rooms with their contemporary style, the public areas at Les Terrasses feel more like part of a home than a hotel. The library is stocked with the latest French novels and interior design books, and also houses Françoise's collection of Moroccan lanterns, tagines and ceramics. The living room, with its low, slouchy, velvet sofas piled high with ethnic cushions, leads through to the intimate dining room, which has windows looking out over the garden on three sides. Tall dressers in the dining room belonged to Françoise's family and are filled with her own ceramics and collection of glasses "from here, there and everywhere".

ABOVE, LEFT A view of the *corralles*, which have been transformed into the guest rooms. They still have a rustic feel, with their wooden barn-style doors and rough stone walls.

ABOVE, RIGHT Lemons from the garden fill a large bowl on a table outside one of the guest rooms.

With her love of good food, Françoise wanted to make high-quality cooking an essential element of Les Terrasses. Beyond an open door in the dining room is the open-plan kitchen. Cream wooden kitchen units and shelves hold glass jars full of spices, tagines and hand-painted ceramics, while stainless-steel worktops and a professional cooker provide essential tools for the chef. A small bright-blue-framed window is set into the wall next to the kitchen door, which remains open to the garden throughout the year. Meals make use of fresh produce from the garden, while the chef's home-made desserts are a speciality. During the summer months, the tables and chairs are brought outside on to the terrace for candle-lit dinners. The mismatched wooden tables and chairs are a mix of local Ibizan pieces from Lorenzina and bespoke designs by André, the in-house carpenter. Françoise has created most of the ceramics in the hotel, making use of her workshop and kiln during the winter months.

Les Terrasses has been one of the most stylish haunts in Ibiza for over ten years. More than just a chic boutique hotel, it is also the place to catch up with the local French community over a cup of coffee and some chocolate madeleines out on the terrace.

OPPOSITE, TOP LEFT AND TOP RIGHT The two chairs covered in green velvet in the living room are from Asiatides in Paris, as is the cast-iron chandelier. A more delicate chair complements a femininely decorated bedroom.

OPPOSITE, BOTTOM LEFT Behind the dining table is a painting by Miquel Buades. The three lamps hanging above the table come from Mia Zia in Ibiza.

OPPOSITE, BOTTOM RIGHT Sculptures based on masks stand on a piano in the corner of the living/dining room.

RIGHT, TOP The handmade ceramic tiles in the bathroom contrast with the contemporary sinks and taps by Philippe Starck.

RIGHT, BOTTOM This feminine bedroom features an embroidered bedcover and a decorative lamp from Lorenzina in Ibiza Town.

cool minimalism

Villa Roca

On an island full of sleek, stylish villas and beautifully designed properties, Angel (Simon Hook) and Flavio Ceccetto decided to construct the ultimate minimalist villa, built into the rocks of the Truntoi mountain range. Villa Roca is 200 metres (650 feet) above sea level, with sweeping views across the island and out to sea, but despite its secluded mountain-top location, the house is only 6 kilometres (4 miles) from Ibiza Town and within easy reach of the island's best beaches.

Someone had already attempted to build a property on the site, but had abandoned the project in the early 1990s. When Angel and Flavio discovered the place, it was completely deserted and vegetation was blocking the road. They knew that it was going to be a challenging project: "It was extremely difficult to build, as the mountain is very steep: as soon as you put something down, it rolls to the bottom, never to be found again." Even finding building contractors was a struggle, because

LEFT, TOP Teak-and-white-faux-leather seating is arranged on the terrace looking out over the salt flats of Las Salinas beach.

LEFT, BOTTOM The dining room opens out on to the terrace (seen from a different angle, top left). Flavio and Angel designed the glass-and-metal dining table and the surrounding seating.

OPPOSITE Sliding floor-to-ceiling windows help to blur the boundary between indoors and outdoors. Hammocks and daybeds invite you to relax outside.

ABOVE, LEFT The rocks of the mountain can be glimpsed through the double-height glass front door.

ABOVE, RIGHT The eat-in kitchen has a mountain backdrop and a sleek modern feel, with recycled teak work surfaces and cupboards, and stainless-steel stools.

it was such a dangerous site: eleven contractors came and went during the three-year period that it took to complete the villa.

Angel and Flavio worked on the design to make maximum use of natural light: floor-to-ceiling windows allow guests to take in the views of the pine forest on the surrounding hills. Flavio is from Brazil, and he imported all the stone flooring for the house from his homeland. The pair designed all the furniture for the rooms themselves, aiming for a sleek and modern look. Their designs were realized locally, from stainless steel, glass, recycled teak and cream faux leather.

The eight bedrooms have an air of calm and tranquillity, with white Egyptian cotton sheets, and monogrammed white towels and bathrobes from BC Software in Britain. Bathrooms are made from the traditional Ibizan polished cement or *marmolina*. In place of sinks, there are bowls of copper or carved white stone resting on concrete plinths. Taps emerge from the wall or appear from curved stainless-steel spouts.

The double-height master bedroom is connected to the living areas by a free-standing white staircase, and contains a bright-red sofa for a splash of colour. The open-plan space also includes the bathroom, with its luxurious circular hydromassage spa bath at the far end and a large curved glass window that opens on to a spectacular view of the forest.

Outside on the terraces, white stone benches and low white tables provide chill-out spots around the house. Smooth terracotta bowls and pots and teak chairs and deckchairs offer a contrast to the otherwise white minimalist feel. Angel and Flavio chose a predominantly white-and-cream colour scheme to maximize the feeling of light and space.

Guests spend a great deal of their time outside on the terraces, enjoying the pool bar and dining area, floating cabana, waterfalls and hidden cave, and a 32-metre (105-foot) swimming pool. Poolside mist systems spray clouds of mineral water to keep summer guests cool. Angel and Flavio have also installed a gym and an infrared sauna.

ABOVE, LEFT The dining room is reached via an elegant flight of steps from the living room. Antique candlesticks and a pair of framed paintings add an elegant touch to the mantelpiece.

ABOVE, RIGHT Floor-to-ceiling windows lead off the main ground-floor living space, opening on to one of the terraces. On another terrace, at the first-floor level, is a large table with bench seating.

OVERLEAF The open-plan master bedroom has a round hot tub set beside the curved window overlooking the pine forest, and a double-height sleeping area that can be screened with curtains for privacy. Angel and Flavio designed the elegant free-standing staircase and white chaise longue specifically for this space.

With its glass-and-stainless-steel table and benches, and curved concrete-and-white-cushioned benches on two sides, the rooftop dining area is a comfortable place from which to enjoy the spectacular views. The dance-floor, Bedouin chill-out tent and hydromassage hot tub that can take up to twelve guests on the rooftop terrace also make Villa Roca the perfect place for wild parties and hedonistic evenings. This is the perfect celebrity hideout, and rock and movie stars clamour to stay here during the summer months. For mere mortals, a better option might be spring, when the hills are carpeted with wild flowers and you can light a fire on chilly evenings.

OPPOSITE Windows in the guest bathroom fold back to create a seamless transition from inside to outside. Made from glass, steel and stone, the bathroom contrasts with the wooden outdoor terrace and the pine forest behind.

RIGHT, TOP AND BOTTOM White stone benches and teak loungers provide the perfect places to relax on the outdoor terraces.

Solibudha

Parisians Jean-Marie Surcin and Philippe Levert decided to leave the stresses of the city behind them and open a guest house in Ibiza. They were hoping to find an existing guest house on the island, to work on together, but eventually discovered a contemporary villa in the countryside and knew that they had found something special. Jean-Marie, inspired by his travels as a make-up artist, worked on the interior design, while Philippe wanted to look after the restaurant and guest house business.

The first room they came across when viewing the property was an open-plan bedroom and bathroom, with a sunken bath and two free-standing sinks made from polished concrete. The interior design was completely different from any of the other houses they had seen, and when they found out that the property was owned by renowned French decorator Bruno Reymond, it all made sense. They have kept the

LEFT, TOP The gardens are dominated by a giant Buddha-head sculpture, which overlooks the swimming pool. The sun sets behind it, forming a dramatic silhouette.

LEFT, BOTTOM The white daybeds and oversized cushions are perfect for relaxing in the evening, while watching the sun set.

OPPOSITE Jean-Marie designed this new minimalist guest room, which is approached through the gardens via a Zen-inspired wood-and-pebble path.

polished-concrete floors throughout, and combined them with white walls and splashes of colour. One guest room has remained entirely as it was designed by Bruno, with a large bamboo bed, and bathroom with a sunken concrete bath and free-standing sink.

Jean-Marie redesigned the terrace, laying down the same concrete floor as inside the house, and added two extra rooms and a new suite by the pool. A stone path leads through the garden to the Japanese suite, which was designed by Jean-Marie to be a Zen-like space. Two rooms are connected by sliding doors, designed, as Jean-Marie explained, to be "a completely peaceful space, with good symmetry between the two rooms".

Every season Jean-Marie and Philippe make changes to their house and guest rooms, introducing new colours, rugs, cushions and sheets. Philippe explains: "Sometimes you don't change a lot, but if you change the little details – the colours, the lamps, the lights – it feels completely different." Two years ago the lounge was Moroccan-influenced and now it is more modern and predominantly white. Jean-Marie often picks up fabric from the Marché St Pierre in Paris and contemporary furniture in Barcelona.

One of the few things that Jean-Marie and Philippe were keen to change at the house was the swimming pool, because they thought it too small. They extended the terrace and built an L-shaped infinity pool. White daybeds and zebra-striped cushions are arranged around the new pool, and white laquered bamboo has been placed in black pots to separate the pool area from the garden. Sculptural palm trees and aloe vera plants echo the carefully designed interiors of the house.

OVERLEAF, LEFT The black-and-white-themed living room is given a splash of colour by the orange rug. The Balinese door, inlaid with mother-of-pearl, leads through to Jean-Marie and Philippe's private rooms.

OVERLEAF, TOP RIGHT A huge painting of the Buddha's face picks up on the 'Solibudha' theme and contrasts with the contemporary Arco lamp by Castiglioni.

OVERLEAF, BOTTOM RIGHT Vases containing aloe vera spikes sit on a striking zebra-print shelf.

Bruno Reymond was so impressed when he saw the redesigned pool area that he presented them with the statue of the Buddha that now sits at the end of the pool. The sun (*sol* in Spanish) sets just behind the head of the Buddha, and the striking silhouette created in the evenings was the inspiration behind the name of the property, Solibudha.

Despite the cool, contemporary design of Solibudha, it has a relaxed, comfortable feel. As well as being a guest house, it is very much Jean-Marie and Philippe's home. Guests often gather in the lounge, or wander into the kitchen as Philippe prepares the evening meal. Solibudha has an ultra-chic style but there are elements of the design that are unexpected and quirky, reflecting the eclectic taste of the owners and creating an unusual environment in Ibiza.

OPPOSITE These sliding Japanese-style doors separate the bedroom from the lounge area in the guest suite. The bedroom has a clean, contemporary feel, with a white platform for the bed, a Philippe Starck bedside lamp and, above the bed, a circular Japanese print, which is illuminated from behind.

OVERLEAF Jean-Marie brought the African masks back from a trip to South Africa. He arranged them on an outside wall to form an installation sculpture, a contrast to the striking shadows cast by a nearby palm tree.

Los Jardines de Palerm

Located in the sleepy village of San Josep, Los Jardines de Palerm is a property with a glamorous past. In the 1930s the house was rented out to the German Dadaist Raoul Hausmann, who lived here with both wife and mistress and shocked locals with his surreal performances in the village square. Can Palerm, as the original house was known, became a stylish hotel in the 1980s, frequented by pop stars such as Grace Jones. Christophe and Cristina Brihet bought the property in 2003, and have transformed it into a contemporary boutique hotel.

Cristina Brihet, formerly a sinologist at the European Commission in Brussels, and her husband, Christophe, a photographer and location manager, initially wanted to build a new hotel from scratch, until they realized how difficult it is to obtain planning permission in Ibiza. When they came across Los Jardines de Palerm, they knew nothing of its history, and simply viewed it as a chic hotel in a south of France style. They set about reinventing it to their own taste. Christophe had strong ideas about light and shade, and came up with the overall concept for the hotel as a haven of cool, restful spaces. The couple chose the colours and shapes together, and Cristina's collection of Chinese manuscripts and ceramics is displayed throughout the hotel.

Cristina and Christophe decided to retain the rustic feel of part of the building, a finca dating back to the seventeenth century, and the rough

LEFT, TOP, AND OPPOSITE Los Jardines de Palerm has two infinity pools. Christophe landscaped the property with low stone walls and sculptural daybeds.

LEFT, CENTRE Rustic Ibizan wooden table and chairs from the 1930s have been placed on the terrace outside the walls of the original seventeenth-century finca.

LEFT, BOTTOM A glimpse of orange blossom on some of the trees surrounding one of the infinity pools.

stone walls with tiny windows and an outdoor oven now form the part of the building with most of the living spaces and the guest suite. Additional guest rooms have been built on, as have the terraces with the two infinity swimming pools. Their modern design produces a striking contrast with the older parts of the hotel.

Christophe created the structural parts of the interiors, with low white walls, polished-concrete floors and built-in daybeds. Cristina picked up bedcovers in Spain, cupboards in Belgium, and the Indonesian chairs came from La Maison de L'Elephant in Ibiza. In the nine bedrooms, she has aimed to create a calm, restful environment; rather than bombarding guests with complicated patterns, she has chosen furnishings that are plain and simple.

When Cristina and Christophe bought the hotel, a friend gave them a pair of chairs that seemed to fit perfectly within the space. Cristina then bought a book about Raoul Hausmann and realized not only that had he lived at Can Palerm, but also that he had had exactly the same style of chairs in the house. In recent years there has been a revival of interest in the Dadaists, and there is now a group of American academics who come to stay here regularly.

The hotel is also famous for its gardens. Cristina explains: "The idea is to let the garden go a bit wild – not to have a perfect garden, but to have the contrast between the wild native plants and the strict lines of the building." Cristina and Christophe have planted numerous indigenous pine and olive trees, and palm trees and fruit trees provide shade on the terraces, with tumbling bougainvillea and honeysuckle, all forming a dramatic setting for this elegant, minimalist hotel.

OPPOSITE The entrance hall has structural low sofas with integral shelves. The table on wheels was from La Maison de L'Elephant. On top of a wooden chest against the far wall is the head of a figure from South Africa, and hanging behind is a work by Richard Long, based on a map of Africa.

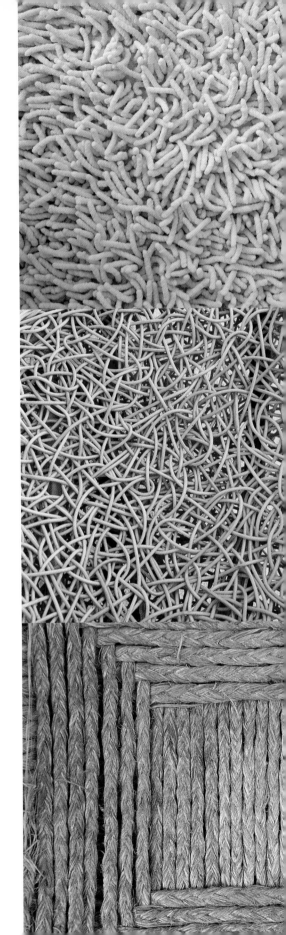

OPPOSITE, BOTTOM RIGHT The table in the dining room is an Ibizan table from the 1930s, which was found in the finca and painted white. The red lamp is from Luz in Ibiza and the wooden chairs are from La Maison de L'Elephant. The organic sculpture is a copy of a pre-Columbian piece.

LEFT, TOP In the bedroom, the low wall behind the head of the bed is used for shelving. The pots to the left are Chinese and the lamps hanging above are from Siempre in Ibiza Town.

LOS JARDINES DE PALERM | 221

Can Tia Den Roig

Parisian couple Peter and Lea Martin both worked in the antiques business, specializing in 'primitive' art, and were keen to find a base in Ibiza. They wanted to build a new house, and began looking for a site on the island in 2000. They found a remote, neglected plot in the rural north, in the middle of a pine forest, from which no signs of habitation are visible for miles. With only a crumbling finca and some ancient terracing on the land, they needed to rebuild the property completely.

Peter and Lea enlisted the help of architect Pascal Cheikh-Djavadi to design their new home, and by 2002 the whole project had been completed. Inspired by the principles of Ibizan landscaping, the architect came up with the idea of creating a series of terraces, alternating smooth white concrete with rough Ibizan honey-coloured stone. Traditional Ibizan architecture, with its cubic shapes, has a similar feel to twentieth-century modernist design, and the new parts of the structure fit well with the old buildings. The thick stone walls of the original square finca lie at the heart of the property, surrounded by a series of linked geometrical rooms. Echoing the building techniques used for the old finca, the pure-white concrete floor was applied by hand to create a smooth surface.

Pascal Cheikh-Djavadi also designed the modernist kitchen, which includes a long central work unit made from white marble, and Ikea

LEFT, TOP, AND OPPOSITE There is an arresting juxtaposition between the original finca made from local stone and the new concrete structure by architect Pascal Cheikh-Djavadi. The swimming pool extends into the landscape from the wide concrete steps that lead down from the living room.

LEFT, BOTTOM The thick concrete walls help to create cool areas of shade. The sculptural-looking openings lead to the bedroom, study and living areas.

ABOVE, LEFT There is an intimate dining area in the corner of the kitchen, with a white table and chairs designed by Eero Saarinen beneath a Verner Panton 'Fun 1' hanging shell lamp, which was designed for J. Luber.

ABOVE, RIGHT In the dining room, architect Pascal Cheikh-Djavadi designed the dark-wood table, which is surrounded by Arne Jacobsen's Series 7 chairs.

cupboards and drawers. At the far end of the kitchen is an informal dining area in space-age white, with a set of the iconic white table and chairs designed by Eero Saarinen for Knoll. Suspended from the ceiling is a mother-of-pearl lamp designed by Verner Panton.

To contrast with the kitchen, the dining room has a long, dark-wood table designed by Pascal Cheikh-Djavadi, surrounded by Series 7 Arne Jacobsen chairs. Antique and modern pieces are mixed together to interesting effect: old glass Indian lamps hang from the ceiling, and vintage Moroccan ceramics are displayed against the wall, next to a 1980s green lamp by Garouste & Bonetti. Cast-iron-framed windows and doors open out onto the garden.

Descending from one of the many different terraces in the house, a large open-plan space leads to the living room, which looks out over the swimming pool to the pine forest beyond. The view can be enjoyed from two dark-grey Alfa sofas by Emaf Progetti, placed at one end of the living

room. Along one wall there is a sideboard from Gandia Blasco, on which is arranged a collection of antique and contemporary artworks. Tibetan drums and African carvings are carefully positioned next to contemporary photographs by Chico Bialas and Antoine Legrand. A pale-blue pot from Greece stands in the corner of the room, adorned with a necklace from Nagaland, north-east India, and juxtaposed with an ancient Roman sculpture.

To offset the cool, white design of the house, Lea likes to introduce bright splashes of colour. In the bedroom, a bright-red Ibizan throw is placed over the bed and a richly textured Moroccan rug covers the floor. Hanging behind the bed are various pieces of interest, including nineteenth-century portraits of four men from New Holland in Indonesia, and necklaces from Nagaland and Africa. Other items in the bedroom include a contemporary pot by Michel Jouanneau and a nineteenth-century Chinese chest.

ABOVE, LEFT Lea chose all the textiles for the bedroom, picking out a contemporary Moroccan rug and a bedcover from Ibiza Town, and made the cushions to her own design.

ABOVE, RIGHT The black cement bathroom for the guest bedroom was made according to an ancient Spanish technique called *cemento pulido*. Peter and Lea's sarongs hang on the wall, above a roughly woven Ibizan basket.

OVERLEAF, LEFT The architect-designed kitchen has a long central unit made from white marble, with a sculptural tap by KWC and Ikea cupboards and drawers. The floor is made from white polished concrete.

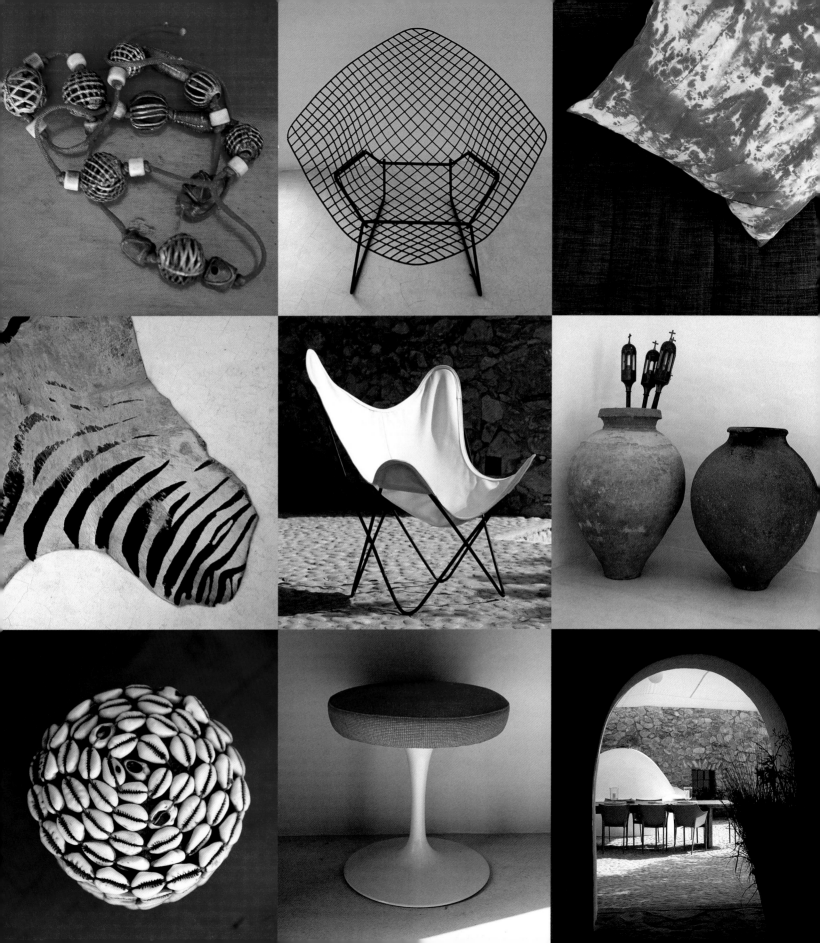

To contrast with the antique feel of the bedroom, the bathroom is cool and modern, with a long, narrow sink and a sunken bath made from polished white concrete. Contemporary fittings chosen by the architect for the bathroom include Axor taps by Philippe Starck for Hansgrohe, and a long, recessed light above the mirror by Agabekov.

The design of the house flows seamlessly from inside to outside, with large windows and doors opening on to the garden and terraces. There is a rustic feel to the outdoor dining area, which is furnished with an old wooden table and Ibizan terracotta pottery. Wooden decking leads out from the living room to the infinity pool. White deckchairs and daybeds by Gandia Blasco are arranged around the pool, with chic white parasols to provide shade.

Rather than being the glaring white modern building, standing out against the landscape, that they could have built, Peter and Lea's new home appears to have grown organically from the terraced hill. The design of the interiors juxtaposes old and new, including 'primitive' art displayed next to European twentieth-century design classics. Outside, this bold contemporary villa makes a dramatic statement but is also sensitively designed to incorporate the old finca and sit comfortably in the surrounding landscape.

OPPOSITE Outside, low seating is shaded beneath a wooden pergola. White cushions are piled on top of a wooden bench, and round rattan floor cushions from Ikea provide extra seating around the low wooden table.

RIGHT, TOP The view from the bedroom window takes in the swimming pool and the pine-forested hills in the distance.

RIGHT, BOTTOM In the living room, a Charles Eames table is placed on top of an antique zebra-skin rug. The dark-grey sofa was designed by Emaf Progetti and the colourful cushions were made by Lea Martin. In the corner is a free-standing Arco lamp from FLOS.

Libela

Xavi Lanau first came to Ibiza when he was twenty years old, to surf the wave of rave culture and go clubbing at Ku, one of the first nightclubs on the island. Twenty years later, he returned with his partner, Alex Estil-les, to look for a suitable site on which they could build a new home. In 2002 the couple met an Ibizan local who was keen to sell off some plots of land, and they encouraged him to show them the more remote parts of Ibiza. They found a quiet valley near Santa Gertrudis, with views stretching across the island to Ibiza Town and the sea beyond, and without hesitation bought the land.

Inspired by the geometry of traditional Ibizan houses, the couple wanted to create a minimalist cube-like design. Now, arriving at the house, all you can glimpse from the road is a white block and a row of palm trees, which runs along an infinity pool. It took over three years for their new home, Libela, to be finished according to their high standards: Alex, director of xxl comunicacion in Barcelona, and Xavi, a photographer, both have a perfectionist streak when it comes to work and home.

The interior of the house was designed to be an open-plan space in which to relax with friends and disconnect from work. Reached via a discreet entrance, the space opens out into a huge double-height living and dining room. Glass walls can be folded away to create one seamless

LEFT, TOP Alex and Xavi designed the elegant loungers that line up alongside the swimming pool.

LEFT, BOTTOM Seen from the lounge area, the infinity pool leads into the view sweeping across the quiet valley below Santa Gertrudis, towards Ibiza Town and out to sea.

OPPOSITE The cubic design of Libela was inspired by the angular shapes of traditional Ibizan fincas. The glass-galleried bedroom is above the living and dining spaces.

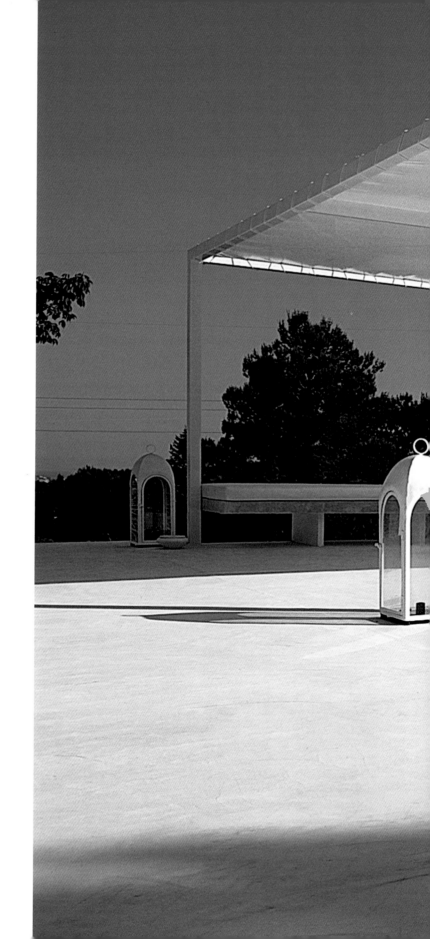

RIGHT The expansive white terrace is used as an additional room during the summer months. The custom-designed white-marble dining table is shaded by a huge awning and surrounded by classic 1960s Verner Panton chairs.

space of the living room and the outdoor area. The architect has carefully considered the position of the house, ensuring that the living room is cool and shady at all times. The predominant colour scheme is black and white, with black slate floors, and black and white furniture including such design classics as the Charles Eames lounge chair and ottoman in the living room. Bright-red and -orange cushions provide flashes of colour.

Spaces for entertaining were also carefully considered, and Alex and Xavi built a professional kitchen to cater for large numbers of guests. Xavi designed the kitchen with Manolo de Brea using Inox materials, with the aim of creating a functional yet elegant space. There are two large Smeg fridges and one Smeg freezer, and a walk-in larder filled with beautifully packaged Spanish products, and rustic terracotta bowls and straw baskets from Tunisia. Alex and Xavi designed their dramatic minimalist dining table to seat twelve people and bought the Philippe Starck chairs from La Maison de L'Elephant in Ibiza.

Steps built into the far wall of the living/dining space lead up to the master bedroom and bathroom, which also has a wall of glass and views over the terrace and swimming pool to the valley beyond. Alex and Xavi wanted their bedroom suite to be very spacious, with two double beds covered with bright-orange throws, a walk-in wardrobe and even a library and study. The bathroom is even larger than the bedroom, with two showers, two toilets, two sinks (all designed by Philippe Starck) and large free-standing mirrors designed by Joaquin Cortes for Habitat.

LEFT, TOP The focal point of the functional white kitchen is the Oxygen Hi-Tech tap from Gessi, which stands at nearly 1 metre (3 feet) high.

LEFT, CENTRE A pair of coffee cups continues the theme of orange detailing.

LEFT, BOTTOM The two doors at the far end of Alex and Xavi's bedroom lead to the dressing room and study.

OPPOSITE The living room is filled with such design classics as this Eames lounge chair and ottoman, and an Arco lamp by Castiglioni for FLOS.

The infinity pool extends from the white concrete terrace, out into the landscape. Alex and Xavi completely landscaped the grounds, and planted palms and aloes imported from mainland Spain. All the outdoor spaces are furnished in white, from the Verner Panton chairs grouped around the marble dining table, to the loungers (made to Alex and Xavi's own design) arranged around the pool. Design decisions were made for aesthetic as well as practical reasons. The outdoor shower, for example, is positioned against the wall of Alex and Xavi's bedroom to benefit from the visual effect of the water against the white building. They also liked the idea of showering, after the beach or swimming pool, "with the sun just above your head".

Alex and Xavi have brought a dash of Barcelona style to Ibiza, mixing classic twentieth-century pieces with their own modern designs, in a contemporary setting inspired by traditional Ibizan architecture. It takes just under an hour to fly from the mainland to Ibiza, which makes this ultra-modern villa the ultimate weekend escape.

OPPOSITE The black slate bathroom has a sunken bath, from which there is a view of the valley. Design details include a large mirror by Joaquin Cortes for Habitat and taps by Philippe Starck.

natural living

Can Blanc

Working as they do in the film industry and often being away on set, Danny and Sophie McGrath realized that there was no need for them to continue to live in London. They had a dream of living in a rural, unspoilt environment with a warm climate, and had specific ideas about what kind of property they were looking for: "We wanted to find something with natural features that we could incorporate into living in a rustic environment, with natural stone that we could use in the garden or in the pool area, or even in the rebuilding of the house."

Unable to find the perfect home, after searching across Spain from north to south, Danny and Sophie booked into a villa in Ibiza over Christmas, curious to see what the infamous party island was really like. As soon as they drove off the ferry, they realized that this was somewhere they wanted to stay and look around, but they viewed fifteen houses a week for two months, without finding one they liked. On their very last day, they were flagged down by a friend who had heard of their quest and whose house had just gone on the market.

Danny clearly remembers his first view of the house: "It was the middle of winter, there were fallen trees all over the place, it was just a wreck, but we knew immediately it was the one that we wanted." What would become their new home was essentially just a shell with

LEFT, TOP A Balinese bench covered with blue cushions and folding wooden chairs around a table create an outdoor eating area. At night Moroccan lanterns illuminate the scene.

LEFT, BOTTOM Just to the side of the organic vegetable garden is a traditional Ibizan well.

OPPOSITE The vivid colours of the outdoor living room were inspired by Morocco. The red-and-orange daybeds and large leather pouffe make a comfortable seating area, which is lit by candles at night.

no electricity and no running water, but they were both so happy to have found it that they did not mind camping while the place was being done up. Danny, with his Scottish background, likened the finca to an old burnt-out crofter's cottage in the Highlands. The previous owners had let the house to a group of Italian trance DJs, and Danny points out, "you can see the painted psychedelic shutters on the front door, which are a hangover from those days".

One of Danny and Sophie's first building projects was to create a new guest room from the old garage, which they called the 'Funky Room'. They replaced the old corrugated-iron roof with a traditional sabina-wood ceiling. Before they restored this room, water used to seep through the mountain rock of the back wall and run across the floor. It now has warm honey-coloured plaster walls, made from natural pigments found in Ibiza, including manganese, ochre and terracotta. Danny made the sabina-wood four-poster bed for this new room and Sophie provided the textiles from

her work in costume design for various films. The couple picked up some wooden carvings and an intricate blowpipe with quiver and darts from a trip to stay with a tribe of Iban (head-hunters) in Borneo.

From the outset, Danny and Sophie were keen to preserve the original stone floors, corner fireplaces and sabina-wood beams. They reconditioned the roof, and all the walls had to be stripped back. A thick layer of caul, a primitive form of plaster traditionally used by Ibizans and made of earth, limestone and water, still covered most of the walls. When this was removed the finca's stonework was revealed. "The stonework we found when we uncovered it all was so beautiful that we decided not to cover it all up again," Danny explains. The plumbing had to be installed from scratch, and the whole building needed rewiring.

Above the windows, the original builders had not made a solid lintel from a piece of wood or stone, but supported the wall with rocks of different shapes tightly wedged together. This was carefully renovated

by the Uruguayan builders, who, says Danny, were "brilliant". Glass windows were fitted where originally there would have been only shutters to cover the opening.

Sophie has found inspiration for her costume designs in the traditional dress of the women in the local village, with their pleated skirts and intricately wrapped shawls, and Danny is fascinated by the Ibizan rituals and festivals. "It's easy for people to think that [it was] the acid-house generation who made Ibiza what it is," he says, "but there have been people partying here for decades, if not centuries, dating back to the Romans and Phoenicians." Sophie and Danny relish the calm lifestyle they have created in their restored, rural finca – their perfect family home.

OPPOSITE, TOP LEFT The traditional-style Ibizan kitchen is decorated in natural warm colours, with earth pigments in the plaster, sabina-wood beams and terracotta floor tiles.

OPPOSITE, TOP RIGHT, AND ABOVE, RIGHT In the 'Funky Room' the four-poster bed is draped with fabrics from Sophie's costume collection and vintage throws. A pair of Indonesian wedding figures sit at the foot of the bed.

ABOVE, LEFT The Moroccan-inspired bathroom has a pair of metalwork-framed mirrors above a blue ceramic sink, which is sunk into a curved, polished wooden shelf. The beach-bag, bikini and kaftan sum up the spirit of outdoor living in Ibiza.

Can Miquel de sa Font

When writer-and-photographer team Anabel and Barnabas Kindersley arrived in Ibiza in 2000, all they brought with them were a few rucksacks filled with their belongings. Together they had travelled through over forty countries but decided on Ibiza as the place where they would settle. They came across an old finca that had been restored some years earlier by the architect Rolph Blakstad. The oldest parts of the house dated back to 1822, and all of the property was in desperate need of some tender loving care. Rolph had not been intending to sell the house, but he saw Anabel and Barnabas as a compassionate and resourceful couple who would respect and restore his old home; and, for their part, they were instantly attracted to the house: "We fell totally in love with its charm and the beauty of it."

It has taken some time for Anabel and Barnabas to create their own style: "We felt like we were buying a house with such a history; it had its own story and it's taken time to make it ours." The layout of the rooms was not very practical for a young family, and the Kindersleys ended up rebuilding the back of the house – with Rolph's assistance – to adapt the living area, bedrooms and bathrooms to their needs. The garden, similarly, "has had lots of love – all the ponds were empty, and now they are filled with water-lilies and frogs".

LEFT, TOP The outdoor terrace is shaded by a roof of sabina beams. Cushioned bench seating and a dramatic Moroccan lantern make this the perfect place for an afternoon siesta or evening drinks.

LEFT, BOTTOM Lavender beds are surrounded by orange trees in the symmetrically laid-out Moroccan-style gardens.

OPPOSITE Two tall palm trees frame a shaded pergola on the far side of the swimming pool. There are lily ponds on either side of the pool.

ABOVE, LEFT AND RIGHT The traditional bench seating, behind the French farmhouse kitchen table, is covered with Anabel's signature pink cushions. The built-in shelving holds ceramic dishes, Moroccan lanterns and cookery books. Just above the table area is an intimate family living room, where they can gather to watch DVDs.

Rolph Blakstad based his designs for the gardens, in particular the geometry of the pool, on the ancient symmetry of the Alhambra palace near Granada. Barnabas has also heard a theory that Rolph planned the exact markings of the garden according to an ancient Egyptian system, using the moon and the stars to guide him. The ancient Persian phrase for such a walled garden, *pairi daeza*, was also used to mean 'paradise', and this magical garden certainly seems to earn that description. Around the pool are marble fountains carved in the style of those at the Alhambra, while wooden carvings from Morocco displayed on the pergola include an Arabic inscription: "If there is paradise on earth, it is here, it is here, it is here."

Sandwiched between Ibizan farmer neighbours, the Kindersleys cannot help but be aware of the changing seasons and the harvests: "The Ibizans have a real respect for nature and the land and how they look after it. Our children have been able to see that: they're so aware of how food is made

and prepared, and how the land is cultivated." The family help their neighbours to dry the figs during the summer months, and take part in the olive and almond harvests in the autumn; they themselves have planted 650 olive trees, which they farm organically. Anabel compares life in Ibiza to their previous, more materialistic life in London: "Living here, that's no longer your focus – not for me, not for the children. We spend a lot more time outside and tending to all the things that need doing. We're just about to pick [the] oranges, to make marmalade." Anabel is an accomplished and enthusiastic cook; she cooks with all the fruit and vegetables from the garden, and even grinds organic flour to make bread and biscuits. Everyone eats in the kitchen, around a huge French farmhouse table, with an Indonesian wooden bench along one side and cosy built-in seating, with bright-pink cushions, along two sides.

The bold colour scheme throughout the house is based around bright pink. Anabel likes strong, bright colours, and found the perfect pink

ABOVE, LEFT The Kindersleys have designed their living room to be a light, airy space, in contrast to the living spaces in many old fincas, which can be quite enclosed and dark. The windows fold back, opening the room to the gardens in the summer.

ABOVE, RIGHT A game awaits completion on one of the strikingly patterned carpets.

hand-dyed silk when she was travelling in Vietnam. The minimum order was 50 metres (154 feet), but she loved the colour so much that she bought it and had it made into fifteen hand-quilted duvet covers and countless pink cushions. These are now dotted around the house, creating strong splashes of colour in all the seating areas.

Friends visit often and can lounge in the living room on huge daybeds covered with kilims, while Barnabas mixes on the decks, casually placed on a large wooden chest. Cushions from India, Morocco and Bali are scattered around the room and Moroccan lanterns are strung from the ceiling. Low tables made from wood and rope are adapted from Indian beds, or *charpois*. In the summer, outdoor seating areas become an extension of the living room, as Anabel describes: "We don't put any furniture outside, we just take the cushions out, and leave them there from April until September. ... the whole house is always open and the outside space becomes in a way an indoor living space. Inside/outside – there's not really much boundary."

Anabel and Barnabas love planning "big trips and voyages in the winter months" with their children, Lily and Max, who are home-educated. Their travels have included Indonesia, Thailand, Vietnam and Bali, and while they are away, they always end up sending "crates of stuff" back for their house. Unlike many of their friends, they have not carefully planned out what the house is going to look like: "What you see in all the furnishings really spells out the way we have lived in Ibiza; we tend to buy things that we like and then try to find a place for them."

RIGHT, BOTTOM The daybeds in part of the kitchen are covered in kilims, creating a relaxed seating area beneath the huge Moroccan lantern.

OPPOSITE, TOP LEFT This intimate sitting room leads off the kitchen. The cushions are covered in pink silk from Vietnam and an Indian *charpoi* is used as a table.

OPPOSITE, BOTTOM RIGHT Anabel and Barnabus's bedroom can be separated from the living room by drawing the white curtain across the arched divide.

Ibiza Moving Arts

Sandra Morrel and Volker Eschmann have been practising contemporary dance and yoga for many years, and when the opportunity arose to take over Ibiza Moving Arts (which Volker first discovered when he was looking for a place to give dance theatre workshops), they jumped at the chance. After years of city living, Sandra and Volker longed for the peace and quiet of the countryside, and bought the property in 2002. Located in a quiet valley in the north of the island, it is the only house for miles around and is deliberately kept discreet.

The couple have seen how yoga, dance and alternative therapies can transform both body and mind, and Sandra feels that many of the guests that stay here "go through a process of change: they want to look inside and learn something about themselves". She believes that Ibiza still has a strong spirit of dance, thousands of years after the Phoenicians were here worshipping their god of dance, Bes.

In the 1970s the owners of the property undertook an extensive project to renovate the house. They kept as much of the old building as possible, and preserved the old stone olive press and wood-fired oven. Many of the stables and outbuildings were converted into guest rooms, and one large building was converted into a yoga and dance studio. When they arrived, Sandra and Volker were keen to make their mark,

LEFT, TOP The entrance to Sandra and Volker's finca is a turquoise, barn-like arched door.

LEFT, BOTTOM During the summer months, the bougainvillea grows up over the wooden trellis to create a shady area outside the living room and bedroom, furnished with a low table and carved Indian chairs and table.

OPPOSITE Beneath a canopy of deep-pink bougainvillea, a white daybed is hung with a mosquito net, creating the perfect place for a siesta.

and one of their first projects was to build a new guest house, or "loft atelier". Volker worked on the designs himself, with the old fincas on the island for reference.

Volker's designs combine contemporary forms with traditional Ibizan building styles. He says: "We wanted it to look like an old finca, made out of stone and the typical Ibizan sabina wood. The glass windows with iron frames were designed to look like the huge windows of a Berlin loft, and we wanted a contemporary look for the bathroom, with Philippe Starck fittings." While constructing the new building, Volker was careful to preserve the one-hundred-year-old dry-stone wall in front of the house, and the old cactus and almond trees beside it. The bathroom window now frames the cherry tree in front of it.

When they moved to Ibiza, Volker and Sandra had very few items of furniture, and brought with them only their most cherished books, paintings and sculptures. Most of the furniture for the new loft studio

was designed by Volker, including the bed, which is now covered with a bright-blue throw from Bassetti in Italy. He also made the hanging rail for clothes, using a rope that he found on the beach, and a stick of Ibizan bamboo called *cana*: "The idea was to leave the guests' clothes visible, so that their colours can add to the atmosphere of the room." The accommodation at Ibiza Moving Arts is self-catering, with a kitchen and dining room in the building next door to the loft for the guests to use. This was originally a stable for sheep but now it is a stylish room, with a French oak dining table from Magazin in Ibiza Town.

With its high ceilings and sabina-wood beams, the living room still has the feel of a traditional finca. Skylights at the far end bring out the colour of a red abstract painting by the artist Gianni Musacchio. The table and mantelpiece display Buddhas and sculptures, collected by Sandra on her travels to India. Over the past twenty years she has built up a collection of books on dance, yoga and meditation, which fills the

bookshelves. Volker has introduced a contemporary touch to the room, with a stylish Italian sofa from Lotus in Ibiza.

The new kitchen combines the traditional design of the old house with such modern elements as kitchen units from Ikea and ceramic pots from Morocco. A brand new sink has been installed next to the old wash sink, and just next to the stove is a door for the old wood-fired oven, still fully functioning. Traditionally, every house would have had an oven like this for baking bread. Such historic items are important to Volker, just as it was important "to keep water and fire in the places where they traditionally were in an old Ibizan home. By preserving these elements, the alchemy of the old house keeps going, and the soul of the place stays alive."

"Here there is so much strong energy," says Sandra, and Volker speaks of the quiet valley as "a strongly transforming place". The couple's positive attitude, the beautiful home that they have created and the relaxing calm of the countryside make Ibiza Moving Arts a magical place to visit.

OPPOSITE, TOP LEFT Behind the hob in the kitchen, an alcove in the wall is just visible: this is the opening to the old wood-fired oven, which is still in use.

OPPOSITE, TOP RIGHT In the entrance hall a vintage chandelier hangs from the sabina-wood beams in the ceiling, and a carved Indian bench offers views out on to the terrace.

ABOVE, LEFT Sunlight from the central courtyard streams into Sandra and Volker's living room. The bookshelves in the alcove in the wall were made with planks of sabina wood. The door in the far wall leads through to their bedroom.

ABOVE, RIGHT The new loft atelier (guest bedroom) was built using traditional techniques, in particular the sabina-wood ceiling. Volker designed the bed to fit the space.

Es Cucons

The Rodriguez Castan family from Barcelona used to spend their holidays in Ibiza, and dreamed of owning a small hotel on the island. Finally, in 1996, Juan Rodriguez and Maribel Castan sent their daughter Maria and her husband, Jaime, to Ibiza to look for a property. The plan was to find an old ruin to restore and turn into a small hotel. They spent a year looking at fincas all over the island, before discovering Es Cucons in the heart of the Corona Valley in Santa Agnes.

Set in the rural north-west, surrounded by rolling countryside, Es Cucons offers wonderful walks through fields full of almond, olive and fig trees. The Corona Valley is particularly famous for its almond trees, which produce clouds of pink-and-white blossom in February and March, and the Rodriguez Castan family were convinced that people would want to discover this other side of Ibiza. They spent three years renovating the property, and opened the hotel in 2000.

The hotel is now looked after by sisters Maria and Barbara, and their partners Jaime Gonzalez Vera and Pasi Kulju. "Our dream," they say, "had always been to live by the sea and in the countryside. It was a challenge to convert this magnificent rural home – dating from 1652 – into a small family hotel." While keeping the Ibizan feel of the building, the family also wanted to add some contemporary touches, such as large terraces,

LEFT, TOP Terraces surrounding the hotel overlook thousands of almond trees in the Corona Valley.

LEFT, BOTTOM Local seasonal fruits and flowers are displayed throughout the gardens, for guests to discover along the paths leading to their rooms.

OPPOSITE This metal-framed daybed is on a private terrace outside one of the suites.

ABOVE This view of Es Cucons shows the terraces outside the guest rooms on the upper floors, which have sweeping views across the valley.

glass doors and big windows, to bring more light into the rooms, and they worked with architect Javier Palleja to update the old building. The family had strong ideas about how the hotel should look, and wanted to preserve the character of the whole property, with its ancient *aljibes* (surface-fed wells), dry-stone walls and natural rock features in the *corralles*.

The design of the hotel is light, airy and comfortable, with a warm, natural style that has been described as 'rustic-chic'. Each room has been carefully put together, with unusual lamps, ceramics and textiles offset by paintings by contemporary artists from Ibiza and Barcelona. To create a romantic mood, beds are draped in muslin, and rooms are decorated with such natural fabrics as silk and linen. All the rooms have been distinctively decorated; some are more Ibizan in feel, with white walls, painted floors and roof beams made from sabina, while others have a Moroccan or a colonial theme.

The Moroccan-inspired guest room features a roll-top bath, placed behind a wrought-iron screen. Painted a rich red, the room is decorated with ochre and granite-coloured silk curtains, a ceramic table and other Moroccan ceramics. To take full advantage of the view, the bed faces the double glass doors opening out on to the terrace, and towards the fertile valley of Santa Agnes.

The restaurant at Es Cucons is known to be one of the best in Ibiza, serving such local specialities as sea bass cooked in Ibizan salt with rosemary olive oil. The crystal chandelier in the dining room is from the Rodriguez Castan family home in Barcelona, and the deep-red walls are hung with local Ibizan paintings and work by family friends, including Xaro and Agustin Fructuoso and Concha Ibanez. The family designed the tables to their own specification, with iron legs and iroko-wood surfaces, and they bought the bamboo chairs from Almacenes Aragon in Santa Eulalia, Ibiza.

ABOVE, LEFT A guest room on the top floor has French windows opening out on to the terrace, which overlooks the unspoilt valley.

ABOVE, RIGHT The daybeds and trees around the pool are hung with chiffon curtains and mirrored beads.

Straw baskets full of oranges, flowers floating in water in rustic stone bowls, and various Ibizan ceramics are artfully displayed around the hotel, and on balconies, terraces and paths. Gardens lead down to the shamrock-shaped swimming pool. There is a glamorous hippy feel to the outside areas, and the romantic lounge beds at one end of the swimming pool, designed by Jaime and Pasi, are hung with mosquito nets from Lotus in Santa Eularia. All the other loungers are from Habitat in Barcelona. The pink curtains and the velvet cushions in white, blue and red were made by Aunt Dora (Maria and Barbara's aunt) and Rosario (Jaime's mother). The pool area is surrounded by trees that are hung with sheer curtains and mirrored beads.

The Rodriguez Castan family have transformed a derelict seventeenth-century finca into the perfect country hideaway. Stylish Ibizan architecture, total attention to detail and excellent food all combine to make this the ideal holiday retreat.

OPPOSITE, TOP LEFT One of the tables in the intimate restaurant, which has traditional Ibizan wooden furniture, crisp white linen tablecloths and paintings by local artists and friends.

OPPOSITE, TOP RIGHT This Moroccan-inspired bedroom is decorated in rich reds and golds.

LEFT, BOTTOM The roll-top bath in the Moroccan bedroom can be screened from the room by a wrought-iron trellis.

Can Marti

Peter and Isabelle Brantschen spent two years exploring Ibiza before they discovered Can Marti in 1993. They wanted to find a comfortable home for their young family, and were attracted to the rural side of the multicultural island of Ibiza. Without much hesitation, they sold their fashion business in Switzerland and moved to Ibiza. When Peter and Isabelle took over Can Marti it had no running water or electricity, but they set about transforming it into an organic farm and hotel. They had to battle with planning regulations to get the place up and running, and finally opened in 1997. Can Marti was one of the first properties in Ibiza to tap into the growing market for environmentally friendly hotels.

The property included a seventeenth-century farmhouse surrounded by outbuildings, and 11 hectares (27 acres) of land. While the surrounding buildings were converted into guest rooms, the family moved into the farmhouse. Peter and Isabelle both like creating interesting interiors and playing around with colours. They wanted the guest rooms at Can Marti to be similar in style to their own living areas, believing that hotels should not be filled with old, unwanted furniture. Despite their love of Ibizan design in general, they were not particularly keen on the local Spanish-style furniture made from heavy, dark wood, and have filled Can Marti with finds from around the world.

LEFT, TOP AND BOTTOM Views of the organic farm and fields of old olive trees, with the pine-forested hills in the background.

OPPOSITE Olivo is one of the guest rooms created from an old *corralle*. It can sleep four people.

ABOVE, LEFT The wooden lattice-style round table and chairs are vintage Mexican pieces picked up at a local antique shop. The natural straw lamp is from Natura in Ibiza.

ABOVE, RIGHT Against the natural stone wall of the house, a metal cut-out sculpture of a cockerel sits on a round metal table, alongside a chair of unpainted metal; all are from Habitat.

The family dining room retains the original flat-stone floor and sabina-wood beams, and a new wood-burning stove from Germany has been installed. The Indonesian wooden chest was picked up on Peter and Isabelle's travels, and the rest of the furniture comes from their old house in Switzerland: chairs from Habitat, an antique wooden table and a piano.

Peter and Isabelle were eager for their guests to feel independent, and designed each room or studio to have its own entrance, plus a kitchen, dining room, living room, bedroom and bathroom. Each guest room has been inspired by a particular country: the converted stable, Olivo, has Moroccan rugs, textiles and furniture, while Almendro, a north-facing studio with wooden steps, has furniture from Rajasthan. Peter and Isabelle have tried to bring back unusual pieces from their travels, including a table and chairs from Mexico for Algarrobo.

Peter tends to spend most of his time working on the farm, while Isabelle takes care of the organic fruit and vegetables. From the kitchen

windows, she has a view out over the farm, while also being able to spot visitors and guests arriving. The kitchen is a mixture of contemporary design and old Ibizan ceramics and baskets, with dried squash, grown from seed in the garden, strung up on one wall.

With the warm, sunny climate in Ibiza it is possible to grow two or even three crops a year. At Can Marti the summer crop includes such typical Mediterranean vegetables as tomatoes, aubergines, peppers, courgettes, beans and cucumbers, and such soft fruits as strawberries and raspberries, while the figs ripen for early autumn. The orchard is full of fruit trees, which yield plums, cherries, apricots, peaches and avocados. Peter admits that organic farming in Ibiza can be very frustrating, as there is "always a new disease, or small animal, which can do a lot of damage". But he has practised organic farming for more than twenty years, and has recently introduced biodynamic methods to the farm.

ABOVE, LEFT Wood found on the beach was first painted and then suspended from rope to create a curtain sculpture to hang in front of an alcove. This was made by a sculptor in Majorca.

ABOVE, RIGHT A built-in concrete bench beneath a tiny window forms the outside seating for the converted stable. For added comfort, there are round rattan mats from Habitat, and brightly coloured cushions.

OVERLEAF, LEFT The traditional Moroccan floor-tiles, in red and yellow, were made with a durable cement base and a thick layer of marble pigment on the surface. The carved and painted wooden table is an antique from Morocco.

The design of Can Marti is as environmentally friendly as possible, with no air-conditioning, television or swimming pool. The Brantschens collect rainwater and recycle waste water, and use photovoltaic energy to make electricity and solar energy to heat water. Guests can cook their own meals with organic fruit and vegetables from the farm shop.

Peter and Isabelle are now part of the local community in San Juan, and their two teenage sons, Tom and Paco, are fluent in Spanish and Catalan. They have made their ambitions come true, and perhaps the greatest compliment that they could have received is the way in which similar agroturismo hotels are springing up all over Ibiza, and elsewhere.

OPPOSITE The main dining room has a vintage cherry-wood table surrounded by rattan chairs from Habitat. Against the far wall is an antique Indonesian sideboard, with a Mondial 2001 poster from Switzerland above. Suspended from the sabina-wood ceiling is a brass Moroccan lamp, between two Murano glass lamps from Magazin in Ibiza.

RIGHT, TOP Olivo is a small stone house, a converted *coralle*, decorated with pieces from Morocco, including an antique painted table, a glass-and-metal lamp hanging from the beams and the red and yellow floor-tiles.

RIGHT, BOTTOM Algarrobo is a Mexican-inspired studio apartment with broad sabina-wood roof beams and a terracotta floor. The brightly coloured bedcovers are from Habitat and the mosquito nets from a local shop.

style directory

hotels

Atzaro (pp. 98–103)
Atzaro Agroturismo, Ctra, San Juan km 15
Tel: +34 971 33 88 38; Fax: +34 971 33 1650
E-mail: agroturismo@atzaro.com; Website: atzaro.com

Hotel La Ventana (pp. 126–31)
Sa Carrosa, 13, DALT VILA 07800
Hotel tel: +34 971 390 857; Reservations tel: +34 971 303 537;
Fax: +34 971 390 145
Website: laventanaibiza.com

Hotel Rural Es Cucons (pp. 262–67)
Santa Agnes de Corona
C/Cami des Pla de Corona 110
Website: escucons.com

Les Terrasses   (pp. 182–91)
Carretera de Santa Eulària km 1, 07840 Santa Eulària
Tel: +34 97 1332 643; Fax: +34 97 1338 978
Website: lesterrasses.net

Los Jardines de Palerm   (pp. 216–21)
Can Pujol d'en Cardona, 34 07830 San José
Tel: +34 971 800 318; Fax: +34 971 800 453
Website: jardinsdepalerm.com

fincas and guesthouses

Agroturismo Can Marti (pp. 268–75)
07810 San Juan
Tel: +34 971 333 500; Fax: +34 971 333 112
Website: canmarti.com

Can Blanc   (pp. 242–47)
Near San Juan
Tel: +44 131 208 1292; Mobile: +34 699 718 311
Website: 23.co.uk/canblanc

Casa Corazon   (pp. 152–59)
Please visit the website for information or to make a reservation
Near Santa Gertrudis
Tel: +34 971 187 178; Mobile: +34 679 340 687
Website: casacorazonibiza.com

Ibiza Moving Arts   (pp. 256–61)
Self-catering accommodation, and yoga and dance workshops
E-mail: info@ibizamoving arts.com; Website: ibizamovingarts.com

Las Banderas   (pp. 60–67)
Playa Mitjorn, Sant Francesc Xavier, Formentera
Tel: +34 666 559 027

Solibudha   (pp. 206–15)
Apartado 160, 07816 San Rafael
Tel: +34 971 345 859; Fax: +34 971 340 098
E-mail: solibudha@gmail.com

villas

Can Reco de sa Bassa   (pp. 72–79)
Website: canrecoibiza.com

Villa Roca   (pp. 196–205)
Tel: +34 68 6351 098
Website: villarocaibiza.com

villa rental and concierge service

Whether you want to make a reservation at a hotel or villa, book
a private chef or yoga teacher, or even hire a private jet or yacht,
contact Deliciously Sorted for a personal concierge service.
Tel (UK): +44 7780 633 225; Tel (Spain): +34 971 197 867
E-mail: info@deliciouslysortedibiza.com;
Website: deliciouslysortedibiza.com

For more information about **Can Canel (pp. 146–51)**, **Casa
Inspiration (pp. 32–39)**, **La Divina (pp. 48–53)** and **Los Patios
(pp. 92–97)**, please contact Deliciously Sorted.

markets

Casi Todo (open March–November)
In this antiques auction house anything goes: on a typical Saturday you might find a tribal mask, an antique hat stand, a 1970s tapestry or a nineteenth-century oak writing desk.
In Santa Gertrudis
Tel/Fax: +34 971 197023
E-mail: casitodo@telefonica.net; Website: casitodo.com

Hipódromo Sant Jordi (9 am–2 pm Saturdays)
Ibizan flea-market, where locals come to sell off furniture, toys, books and clothes. It is a great place to find a bargain.
Carretera Ibiza-Aeropuerto s/n, Baleares 07800
Tel: +34 971 39 6669

Mercadillo de Las Dalias (11 am–7 pm Saturdays; summer only)
Ibiza's hippy market sells clothes, bags and jewellery. This is the place to get a henna tattoo or a glass of mint tea. Christmas and Epiphany (January 6) are special market days.
Carretera de San Carlos, San Carlos, Baleares 07800

interior design and clothing

100% Ibiza
Specialist shop for customized tipis (see, for example, Serena Cook's, pp. 86–87).
Near Santa Eularia
Tel: +34 971 331 596

Becker Interieur & Design
The most stylish interior design store in Ibiza.
Carrer Venda de Parada 6, Santa Gertrudis 07814
Tel: +34 971 197 737

Deseo (open May–September)
Find kaftans, paintings, sun-dresses and hand-painted wooden shoes here.
On Benirras beach, in the north-west of Ibiza, in between San Juan and San Miguel.

Ganesha
Kate Moss, Elle Macpherson and Jade Jagger love the handmade silk kaftans, original Pucci and Chanel dresses, vintage accessories and furniture from the 1950s to the 1970s.
Montgri, Ibiza Town
Tel: +34 971 193605

La Maison de L'Elephant
This is where to come for the Ibiza look: huge white daybeds, statues of the Buddha, Philippe Starck furniture, and more.
La Maison de L'Elephant Ctra. – San Antonio, 2 km
Website: lamaisondelelephant.com

Lorenzina Decoration
Glamorous store that sells bohemian-style four-poster beds, customized cushions and bedcovers, eclectic lamps and ceramics.
San Juan, km 4.5 (Sta. Eulalia road), Jesus 07819
Tel/Fax: +34 971 19 02 55
Website: lorenzina-ibiza.com

Natura
Aníbal, 8, La Marina 7800
Fair-trade shop in Ibiza Town that stocks clothes, furniture, candles, blankets and bedcovers.

Sabama
Locals come here to stock up on chic furniture and vintage pieces for the home.
Carretera de San Juan, km 3, Baleares 07819
Tel: +34 971 19 1924

acknowledgements

We should like to thank all the Ibiza residents who so generously
gave up their time to be interviewed and photographed. We are
very grateful to them for opening up their homes to us and
revealing a new and unexpected side of Ibiza. We would have
been lost without Patrick Kinmonth and Grillo Demo, who
introduced us to Ibiza's most stylish inhabitants.

Thanks also to our families and friends, who supported us
throughout this project. We'd especially like to thank Paul Franklyn,
Kerry Olsen, Serena Cook, Vincente Hernandez (for good times at
Ganesha), Valerie Smith (for English tea and sympathy) and the
lovely Kindersley family.

At Merrell we are most grateful to Hugh Merrell and Julian Honer
for enthusiastically embracing *Ibiza Style*. Special thanks are due
to the Merrell team, in particular to our editor, Helen Miles, to
Paul Shinn in the design department, and to Sadie Butler in the
production department. Thanks also to Martin Lovelock, the
book's designer.

Finally, we should like to thank Molly Timmis, one of the
original Ibiza pioneers, for having the vision to buy a stylish
1950s apartment overlooking the ocean, and her daughter Anne
Rasmussen for letting us stay there and create our own *Ibiza Style*
nearly half a century later.

First published 2007 by Merrell Publishers Limited

Head office
81 Southwark Street
London SE1 0HX

New York office
49 West 24th Street, 8th Floor
New York, NY 10010

merrellpublishers.com

British Library Cataloguing-in-Publication Data:
Rasmussen, Ingrid
Ibiza style
1. Interior decoration – Spain – Ibiza Island 2. Interior decoration – Spain – Ibiza Island – Pictorial works
I. Title II. Grimshaw, Chloe
747'.0946756

ISBN-13: 978-1-8589-4362-6
ISBN-10: 1-8589-4362-0

Produced by Merrell Publishers
Designed by Martin Lovelock
Copy-edited by Kirsty Seymour-Ure
Proof-read by Elizabeth Tatham

Printed and bound in China